NOTEWORTHY
PARENTING

How to Use Your own IDEAS to Create Your PARENTING ROADMAP

CHEERS TO YOUR PARENTING JOURNEY!!

→

BEGIN!!

KRISTIN BUCHTEL

KRISTIN BUCHTEL

Noteworthy Parenting: How to Use Your Own IDEAS to Create Your Unique Parenting Road Map
Published by Booktell Press
Denver, CO

ISBN: 978-0-578-55438-9

FAMILY & RELATIONSHIPS / Parenting

Cover and Interior design by Victoria Wolf

QUANTITY PURCHASES: Schools, companies, professional groups, clubs, and other organizations may qualify for special terms when ordering quantities of this title. For information, email Kristin@noteworthyparenting.com.

This book is printed in the United States of America.

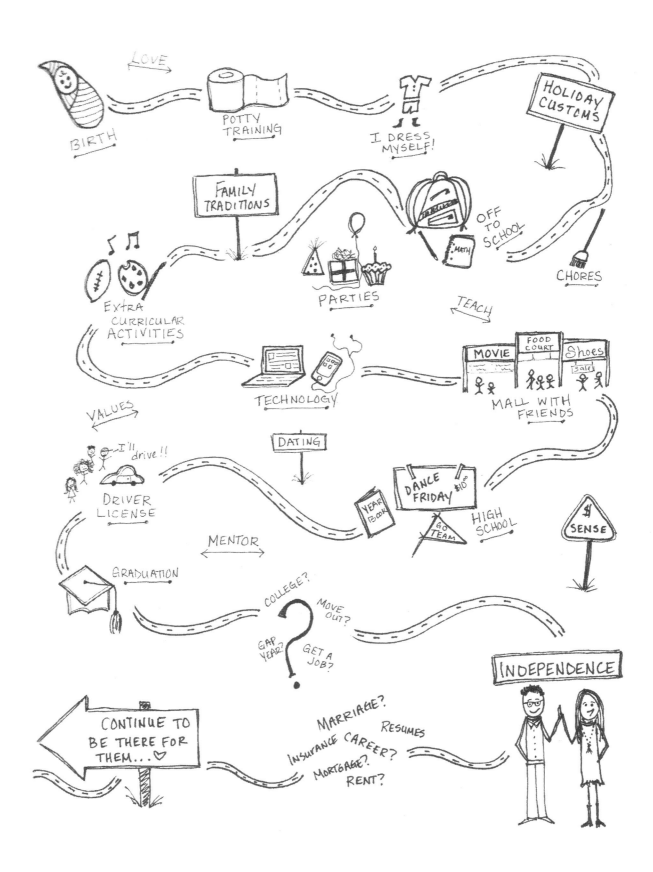

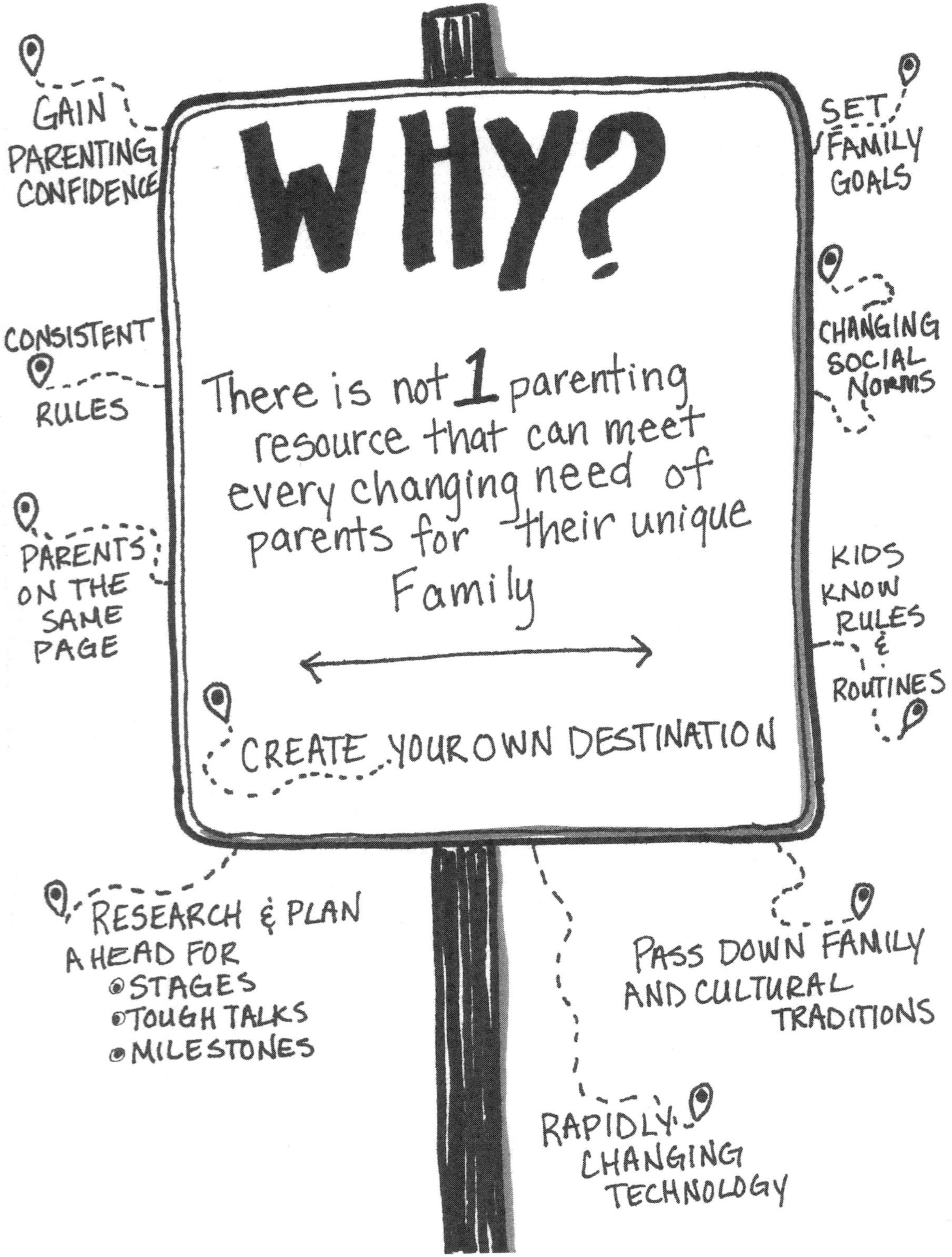

WHY?

There is not **1** parenting resource that can meet every changing need of parents for their unique Family

⟷

CREATE YOUR OWN DESTINATION

GAIN PARENTING CONFIDENCE

SET FAMILY GOALS

CONSISTENT RULES

CHANGING SOCIAL NORMS

PARENTS ON THE SAME PAGE

KIDS KNOW RULES & ROUTINES

RESEARCH & PLAN AHEAD FOR
- STAGES
- TOUGH TALKS
- MILESTONES

PASS DOWN FAMILY AND CULTURAL TRADITIONS

RAPIDLY CHANGING TECHNOLOGY

To my husband and four kids, who have made
my parenting journey noteworthy.

Table of Contents

INTRODUCTION

"If I screw up raising my kids, nothing else matters much."
— Tom Baker, *Cheaper by the Dozen*

This is the book I wish I would have been handed as I left the hospital over twenty-five years ago. I had my firstborn in one arm and was handed a folder of printouts for the other. The nurse gave me a pat on the back and wheeled me out the front door.

It was overwhelming.

That first click of the car seat in the hospital driveway meant we were officially heading out into the world as parents. She was so tiny. We were so worried. I rode in the back seat with her while my husband chauffeured us home.

We settled into the house, sorted the paperwork, and began a notebook of her eating and diapering schedule, as we were told. My husband's notetaking rivaled that of a PhD scientist. He kept it up until the pediatrician chuckled and said we could stand down on the notetaking after our two-week visit.

We went on to have three more kids. Three more chauffeured rides home, and three more notebooks of infant eating and diapering updates. While the diaper notetaking cut down a lot, life was still chaotic. Was it just us? Were we the only exhausted, overwhelmed parents? So much to learn, so much advice, so much gear.

We loved our big family, but there had to be a better way to parent than by the seat of our pants. That's how we managed, until one day while driving through Iowa on our way home to Denver, our perspective changed.

We had been on vacation with a group of old friends and their young families in Chicago. The kids in the group ranged in age from preschool up to middle school. All the parents shared their stories of family life as we herded the kids through the Chicago sites. Each family seemed to be fighting similar battles, whether they were with discipline, homework, or just an overall frustration with busy family schedules.

There just had to be a better way, but what could that be?

On the drive home, I stared out the window, watching cornfield after cornfield go by. I started to reminisce about what family life was like when I was a kid.

The rules and consequences were clear.

There was not as much technology accessible to kids and families then.

Life seemed straightforward and simple as long as you worked hard in school and followed the rules.

Then I started to think about what was ahead for our family. Middle school was right around the corner for our oldest, which meant we were on the brink of the teenage years. The four-year gap between the two oldest and the two youngest made it hard to remember and parent in the same way as we did for the older two kids.

As the cornfields continued to roll by, I brought up the subject with my husband and mentioned a few of the rules and systems from my teenage years.

I had to get a job to save for my first car. I had a curfew of 11:30 p.m. My parents paid for my college education.

Then my husband commented that he was involved in a lot of activities at school and that he never had a curfew. His parents bought his first car. He had to pay his own college tuition.

We both realized how different our experiences were growing up, but where would we go from here? What were our systems and rules going to be moving forward? How were we going to create a parenting plan for all the new technology and social changes that have occurred since we were teenagers?

The kids seemed happy and occupied buckled in the back of the van, and we were able to continue our conversation. A plan started formulating as we began to agree upon systems, rules, and consequences. I grabbed a notebook and pen from the back seat and began taking notes of all our ideas. Some of the items we started with were:

- A ten- to fifteen-hour job in high school
- Kids pitch in for a car and gas money
- A few curfew rules

The ideas covered topics from holiday events to chores. By the time we hit Denver, we not only had a packet of ideas, but we felt like we were on the same page with a plan in hand. We felt confident and excited about the upcoming teenage years instead of dreading them.

Later, we typed and saved the notes on our family computer so we could refer back to them. I now call it our Parenting Roadmap.

Over the years, my husband and I used our Parenting Roadmap:

- As difficult topics would come up
- To write down good ideas as we observed them
- To keep notes about helpful chapters in books
- To reference websites
- To adjust our notes as needed

Our roadmap may be rough to look at, and a little messy; however, it has been our parenting compass. It is our own unique parenting plan.

As parents, we are all coming from different past experiences and have various examples of how to parent. Creating the roadmap together allows each parent to have input. It allows parents to discuss what their system should be and use their gut instincts to develop plans that feel right to them. Once the plans are laid out, parents feel empowered with confidence.

They say there is no instruction manual for becoming a parent, but I would like to think that this book is a good start in the right direction. As adults, we spend a lot of time planning for our lives. We make lists, budgets, and spreadsheets for things like groceries, taxes, and college.

Why don't we take the time to plan out our thoughts about how we're going to raise our kids and prepare them for adulthood?

In its simplest form, the Parenting Roadmap is a collection of "notes to self" for your parenting.

Let's begin creating your Parenting Roadmap!

HOW TO USE THIS BOOK

"The secret to getting ahead is getting started."
— Mark Twain

To get ready for this journey, I recommend having a few office supplies on hand and familiarizing yourself with the icons listed in this section.

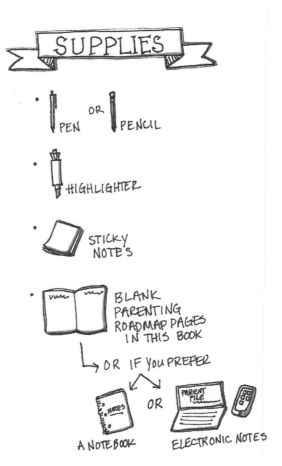

SUPPLIES

Using this book requires more than just reading. To get the full benefit of the chapters that follow, you need to take notes actively. Have supplies ready to jot down your ideas, highlight valuable sections, or even dog-ear some pages. Write in the book! Highlight the good parts you want to remember. Use sticky notes to bookmark pages. It is a tool for you as you begin to formulate plans for your Parenting Roadmap.

Next, think about where you want to write and document your Parenting Roadmap. You may prefer to use:

- A separate notebook

- A notetaking phone app

- Electronic files on your computer

- Or, of course the official companion guide, the Parenting Roadmap Journal, see more on page 164.

Make sure it is accessible for all parents and guardians involved so that anyone can reference it or add to it as needed.

The feel of your Parenting Roadmap is similar to that of an old family recipe book. There may be recipe cards taped into the book, or handwritten adjustments to special recipes. Some pages are bent or bookmarked. If you opt for an electronic file, you may have articles cut and pasted into sections, or snippets of emails or blog posts that you can refer back to. It may not look pretty, but the notes and information inside are valuable and useful for you, and maybe the next generation too.

To keep your roadmap easy to use, you may want to have sections or create separate folders for different ages. I suggest:

- Infant
- Toddler
- Preschool
- Primary Grades (K–2)
- Secondary Grades (3–5/6)
- Middle School
- High School
- Young Adult

I do recommend a few other categories later in the book, but these will get you started.

ICONS

 This Food for Thought Exit road sign is like a pitstop. It relates a story or idea to the topic being discussed. Each Food for Thought Exit will be numbered and labeled, and they are indexed in the back of the book so you can easily look them up later if you want to refer back to them.

 This Notes icon shows up as a reminder to stop and take notes either on the page, in the back of the book, or wherever you are taking notes!

 This Resources icon shows up throughout the book when a helpful book or website is recommended.

CHAPTER 1

Start Your Roadmap with IDEAS

"Creative thinking inspires ideas. Ideas inspire change."
— Barbara Januszkiewicz

Parenting is hard.

Technology changes. Society changes. Parenting must change as well to keep up with the times.

Let's start with the IDEAS process to create your Parenting Roadmap and change the way we look at parenting.

Parenting is a unique experience in each family. There is great diversity between each human being, and therefore, each family raises kids uniquely.

No two parenting roadmaps will be identical.

Throughout your parenting career, you will use all or parts of the IDEAS process over and over to develop your parenting strategies, or to tweak them and add to them.

Once you get the system down, you won't be thinking about what you are doing as you proceed on your journey. It's like learning to ride a bike! As the process becomes more natural, you will be able to develop a plan faster than you did in the beginning.

I   **Imagine Concerns**

D   **Develop Strategies**

E   **Enlist Others**

A   **Author Your Roadmap**

S   **Solutions for Noteworthy Parenting**

Setting an appointment with your spouse or parenting team is necessary to get started. Then set up appointments with each other to check in and see how things are working or if you need to add to or update any areas. How often should you meet? You choose! Once a quarter? Every week? Twice a year?

IMAGINE CONCERNS

The best place to begin is where you are right now.

Are you expecting your first child? Do you have children already?

Start where you are. If your kids are in elementary school, begin with those ages and move forward from there. If you are not yet a parent, then you get to start from the beginning.

☑ Schedule it!!

INFANT   HIGH SCHOOL   TODDLER   EXPECTING   8 YEAR OLD   7TH GRADE

Imagine your parenting style.

Are you strict or more of a softy? What boundaries and routines can you set up to help things run smoothly?

Reflect on your childhood and how you were raised. Which traditions and activities would you like to pass on to your kids? Which favorite holiday customs? Which childhood bedtime stories? Which hobbies?

Next, imagine what life skills you would like to teach your kids. Managing money, time, and household responsibilities are good skills to start thinking about.

Do you have goals that you would like to set for your family? Maybe you would like to take the family to Europe, attend a Cubs game in Chicago, or hike the Grand Canyon. You may have a family goal to do a service project in a third-world country or participate in a 10K charity race. How can you think about breaking big family goals into smaller planning steps to make the goals attainable?

Begin imagining how you want to prepare for milestone events such as starting school, driving cars, graduations, or weddings.

Begin to get a feel for your parenting goals and comfort zones.

MIDNIGHT WORRIES

Worry often goes hand in hand with parenting. The worst of worry shows up in the middle of the night when we imagine our parenting concerns and we cannot sleep.

- How can I help my sick baby feel better quickly?

- Why is my child struggling with reading?

- Who is the bully that is picking on my kid?

- I need to plan the birthday party.

- Why isn't my teenager home yet?

- How will we afford college?

The thoughts start reeling on and on. You begin to imagine worst-case scenarios. How will you ever get back to sleep?

The middle of the night is not the time to make big parenting decisions, although it is the one time that you probably won't be interrupted by the kids.

Keep a notebook, pen, and a flashlight on your bedstand. When you wake up with a worry or a great parenting idea, you can write it down and go back to sleep. Your notes will be ready for you to revisit in the morning when

 you can think clearly and share your thoughts together as parents to find solutions or implement a new idea.

If you are starting to imagine topics for your Parenting Roadmap, take a minute and start writing them down.

DEVELOP STRATEGIES

Now that you have imagined concerns that you would like to address, you can begin to develop strategies. Using your list of parenting concerns, start brainstorming, observing, and researching to create options and answers.

Be ready to negotiate solutions with your parenting team or start to decide which solutions suit your parenting styles, goals, and traditions.

In this section, I will define how to use brainstorming, observation, and research to find or create your strategies.

If you already have strategies or know what your system will be for certain situations, then go ahead and write those notes in your Parenting Roadmap.

Anytime you need creative solutions or maybe a few different strategies to choose from, this is the section to revisit.

BRAINSTORM

Brainstorming is the act of writing every idea on a chart and then weeding through to find the best ones. It's that simple. You will have a parenting issue that may require unique thinking. You can create your own answers to solve a problem.

With the rapid changes in technology and constant social changes that occur today, brainstorming is a great strategy for parents. Today's parents must face many topics that were not faced by previous generations, and they must create solutions along with the changing times. Check out Chapters 4 and 5, The Ever-Changing Technology Climate and The Ever-Changing Social Climate, for a more in-depth look into both of those topics.

ONLINE SHOPPING

The introduction of online shopping has been one of the greatest conveniences I have enjoyed as a parent. Looking back, I may even have been a bit addicted to waiting for those packages to show up

on my doorstep. I was a regular on Amazon.

One day, however, an Amazon package showed up for our middle school son. Hmmm . . .

- What was in that box?

- How was he able to place an order at his age?

- Did he get ahold of my credit card or my account passwords?

- Aren't there age restrictions for buying online?

- Was the content in the box appropriate for his age?

I had no idea that he could set up an account to shop online. I asked myself, *What should the privacy boundaries be? Do I need to set up a formal inquiry or grab a box cutter and tear that sucker open?*

When my son arrived home from school, I showed him that box and was ready to ask all of my questions, but he just started opening the box in front of me.

The contents ended up being a videogame, and he had purchased it with a gift card.

Harmless enough, but I still did not feel comfortable with him accessing anything and everything that could be purchased on Amazon. I felt he was at an age that I did not want him buying games or movies that had inappropriate content. This eventually was also a concern I had about purchases the kids made through the Apple iTunes store.

The situation left a parenting gap for us to sort out. My parents had never had to deal with online shopping, and this was a new parenting issue that required brainstorming.

We began by making sure our accounts were connected to the kids' accounts. This did end up causing a lot of heartache with my Apple ID down the road, but at the time, we thought it was best for me to share an account with the kids. To this day, a Miley Cyrus or Justin Bieber song will pop up in my shuffle mode.

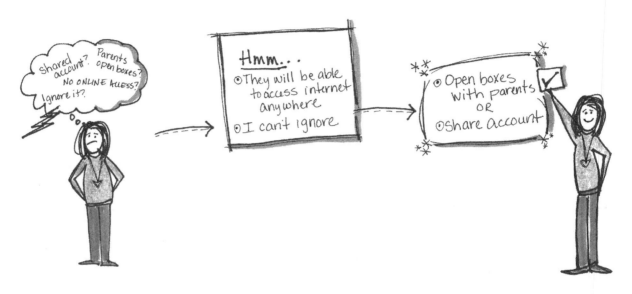

Several apps and software programs can help parents control and monitor their kids' online purchases and streaming, which help, but parents still have to be vigilant. What will your plan be for online shopping and streaming for your family? At what age will your kids have shopping, streaming, and subscription access? How will you help them manage their money online?

OBSERVATIONS

What do parks, restaurants, and movies all have in common? They are great places to observe families. All around us, parenting is happening. People around the world have behavior and interactions on display that we can learn from.

You can see how many opportunities there are to observe parenting:

- Malls
- Restaurants
- Amusement parks
- Hotels
- Offices
- Churches
- Hiking paths
- Elevators
- Hospitals
- Schools

You can also observe and learn from actors portraying family life in TV shows, movies, and plays. You can gain more in books and even on social media.

Sit back and take a closer look.

- What is happening in a particular situation?

- Are they disciplining?

- Are they teaching?

- Are they patient, angry, or frustrated?

- How are they solving a problem?

- Are their methods effective or not?

- Would you do it the same way or differently?

Most importantly, what insight can you take away for your own parenting?

Put yourself in the shoes of the people you are observing and try to learn from them.

Let's practice. Think of spending a nice day at the park. Kids love trips to the park, but what happens when it's time to leave? Maybe your kids leave without a fight, but it is common for kids to become upset and angry when it is time to go.

If you were at the park on this day, you could walk away with two excellent strategies:

1. Give the kid(s) a heads up that you will be leaving in a few minutes.

2. Set a timer, which is a great signal to the kids that it's time to go.

AIRPORT TREATS

Another great place to observe parenting is at airports. Recently, my daughter and her husband were at the airport, queuing up to board a plane. They did not have children yet, but were observing a family who was preparing their little ones for the flight.

The parents handed sacks of treats to each child. The treats were little games and toys, clearly meant to keep the kids occupied on the long flight!

My daughter and her husband noticed how excited the kids were. They tore through each little trinket in the bags. What a great idea for keeping them busy on the flight.

As it was time to walk on the plane, however, the kids were done and bored with the toys. What was the plan for those parents now?

The wisdom my daughter and her husband walked away with was that the treat bags should be given on the plane and to spread out the treats over the course of the flight. They shared the story with me as I was beginning to write this book. It may be the first entry into their Noteworthy Parenting Roadmap.

Not every public interaction you see, or every movie you watch will have relevance to your parenting. However, it's interesting how you run across an episode of your favorite show or see an interaction in public that is noteworthy for your situation.

Those are the golden moments to ponder or create a "note to self." If there is good wisdom to take from the situation, or it sparks a great idea for your own parenting, then use it. If it is a negative situation, how would you do things differently to avoid the mishap?

RESEARCH

Parents, there is no one book, class, or system that has all the parenting answers. Why? Because each family consists of parents who grew up having different experiences, and each child in a family is unique.

As of the writing of this book, there are nearly 80,000 listings for parent books on Amazon.

You may already know that there is an abundance of information out there on parenting. You can follow blogs, check websites, take classes, and attend seminars.

These days, parents can be overwhelmed with tips and advice on the best ways to do their job.

Parents, only you know what you and your kids need. The key is to focus on the research that is pertinent to your needs.

For example, if your child caught on quickly to toilet training, then you do not need further research on this topic for your roadmap, unless, of course, you anticipate a difficult time with a younger sibling.

If a discipline guru has sound advice that suits your personality, then follow that system, but remember it's okay if you find yourself unable to follow the program 100 percent of the time. Make it your own.

As you come across parenting topics that you need more information for, you may want to ask other parents you know to see if they have suggestions for great sources of information. They may have done a lot of research already and can give you a head start.

Save the gems of advice you find and add them to your notes. Add reference information in case you need to revisit that resource later.

If you are reading a parenting book, grab your highlighter and sticky notes to mark pages you may want to look back to, just like you are doing in this book. Write the best takeaways in your Parenting Roadmap. As a parent, you will not have time to go back and re-read books, so when reading for the first time, make the most of it and take notes!

You may find one parenting book has a valuable chapter for what you need help with, but the rest of the book is not your style. That is great because you are the boss. Use what works, and don't mess with the rest.

There's no need for hours and hours spent online on research as if you were going to write a thesis on parenting. Simply take the areas where you need a little more information, find a few good sources, and add them to your Parenting Roadmap.

KIDS' GROWING AND CHANGING BODIES

Sometimes you can find the best advice and help in books for kids. I found great resources in simple children's picture books.

Around third grade, our pediatrician recommended talking with our oldest about the puberty changes that were ahead. Kids were hitting puberty at earlier ages, and it was time to start a basic dialogue on the subject.

 In my search to find resources to help me talk with my daughter, I found The Care and Keeping of You 1: The Body Book for Girls published by American Girl. This book was perfect!

I used the book to help me prepare what I wanted to say. I put sticky notes on pages I would review with her later as she continued to grow. I used the pictures and diagrams in the book to help explain the different topics I wanted to cover at the appropriate times.

One topic we discussed was about getting her period. This first book goes over what a period is and how to use a sanitary pad. The book introduces what tampons are, but the book for older girls, The Care and Keeping of You 2: The Body Book for Older Girls, which I purchased later, gives more details about how to use tampons.

I held onto the books, as we had three younger kids in the house who were not ready to run across this information, but my daughter knew that anytime she had a question, we could talk and we could get the book out if needed to help answer her questions.

 For the boys, there is a similar book called The Boy's Body Book. It is similar to the books used for girls.

All three books covered many topics, such as:

- Hygiene care (deodorant, shaving)

- Bodily changes to expect

- Emotional changes

- How to feel comfortable asking questions and talking about their changing body

- Social situations

Even though these books were written for kids, they are the perfect fit for helping parents talk with their kids!

ENLIST OTHERS

Parenting is not about keeping up with the Joneses but teaming up with the Joneses.

The creation of this roadmap was not only useful to my husband and me, but useful to other parents we know.

Often, we would talk about our family at dinners or in the workplace. When parenting topics would come up, sometimes we would mention the collection of parenting notes we had compiled.

People wanted copies of our roadmap so they could put together their own Parenting Roadmap. We shared what we had with others, and they helped us as well because we would take their ideas and add them to our notes!

PARENT NIGHT OUT

The Parenting Roadmap is an excellent tool, but what also enhances your parenting is when you develop a network of parents or support group to share ideas with. You can start to develop that network at:

- PTA meetings
- T-ball games
- Churches
- Work
- Any place that you meet other families

A parenting network helps reduce the stress and anxiety of parenting by sharing your struggles and celebrations with people who are going through similar experiences.

It is like having your personal think tank. You can get different ideas, strategies, and perspectives from each other.

GROUPS OF FRIENDS OR CO-WORKERS

TEAM PARENTS

Maybe you are researching the latest smartphone technology, the safest family car for new drivers, or the best method to teach kids how to tie shoes. A lot of information exists out there. Ask around.

Maybe your neighbor purchased the latest smartphone and they have hands-on knowledge of all its capabilities.

Maybe as you're sitting in the bleachers at your kid's high school game, you overhear a conversation about what kinds of cars other parents on the team use for their new drivers.

Maybe while standing on the playground waiting for your child to get out of school, you ask other parents how they taught their kids how to tie shoes.

All this parenting advice can come from your parenting network.

Then there are times when we may need to enlist others to help with a behavior issue.

Your daughter is relentlessly demanding the newest over-marketed dolly. Your strong-willed son has traded in doing homework for video games again. Your teenager just got their second speeding ticket.

You have tried lecturing and grounding, and maybe you have even lost your cool a few times. Nothing is working.

Is anybody else dealing with these issues? Do they have ideas that are working for them?

Yes!

Other parents are going through the same things you are.

Other parents have creative and unique ideas to share with you.

Other parents may have the same struggles and have found no answers yet, either, but by collaborating, you can all create solutions.

Getting help from other parents helps you to regroup, try a new strategy, or just regain your strength to stay consistent with your current methods.

I NEED HELP FOR A SICK BABY!

It all started with a bout of diarrhea. My grandson was not his usual energetic eight-month-old self. He was subdued and starting to develop a diaper rash. My daughter and son-in-law were monitoring him but beginning to worry.

The diarrhea continued and prompted a visit to the doctor the next day. The doctor recommended using an oral electrolyte drink to help avoid dehydration and to keep observing him for worsening signs of dehydration. Of course, if things did not get better, he would need to come back for a re-check.

Later in the day while visiting me, he started vomiting. Of course, this started after the doctor's office had closed for the day. We cleaned up the mess and began working on a strategy.

My daughter began enlisting advice. She asked me what we should do about his feedings, and I remembered that he needed to go about an hour before we could give him any more electrolyte solution. I thought we should hold off on formula and food for a bit.

She proceeded to text two of her friends with babies at similar ages. They both had already experienced a tummy bug with their babies and had so much helpful advice.

They suggested to avoid formula or food for eight hours while giving the electrolytes, monitor how many wet diapers he had, and to check for fever. If he stopped having wet diapers or his fever got worse, she should call the after-hours number for the doctor.

She then remembered what she had heard from her aunt about giving sick kids the electrolyte solution a little at a time with a syringe instead of using a bottle.

Then she recalled that her sister-in-law had set up a "well station" recently when her kids were sick. The well station had all the medicine and gear needed to care for her sick child in one spot in her house, keeping all the items and medicines handy, and setting herself up for success.

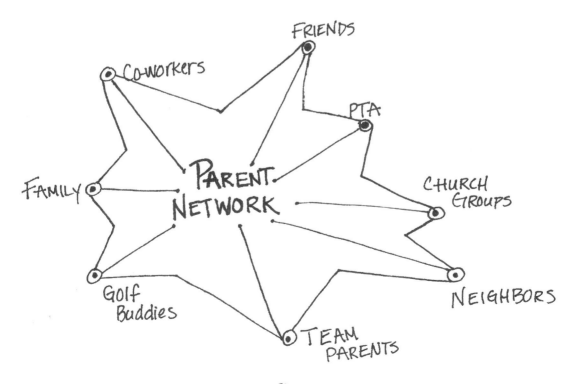

By enlisting the help of her parenting network, she was confident she knew how to care for her son overnight until she could reach her doctor. Of course, if things worsened, she could call the after-hours number.

Sometimes parents need specialized groups to support their parenting. They may have kids with disabilities, diseases, mental illness, or special learning needs.

They may receive special services but could really use a community of other parents whose children are experiencing the same issues.

These children and their families may have many financial and legal needs. In these instances, it is good to have a parenting network or support team with other parents experiencing the same needs. Parents who don't fall into this category may have a difficult time understanding how to help those who do.

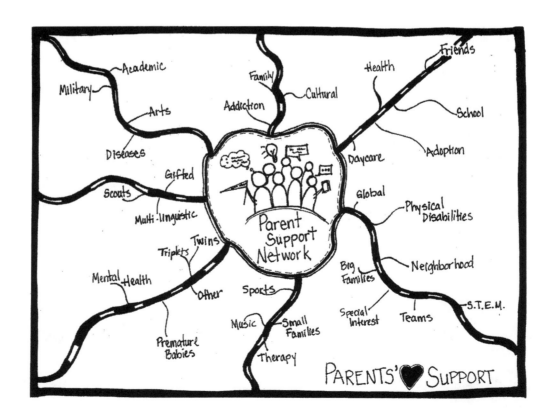

Many support networks are out there for the special needs of these families, and the networks can be recommended by doctors, psychologists, and social workers. If you fall into this category as a parent, check out support groups that could help you. You may also be able to educate other parents who would like to offer their help to you.

Just a reminder, if the parenting issues you are facing would be embarrassing for your child if you shared them with others, you should seek the help of a pediatrician or therapist. Maybe your child is wetting the bed at an older age—your doctor may be the best resource for advice. Some issues may be too embarrassing for your child if you are sharing them with other people.

Having a group of parents that you can talk to and get help from is a great asset to any parenting team.

 Who is in your parenting network? Where can you find more parents to network with?

Author your roadmap

You are the author of the roadmap, and it is not intended to be a literary masterpiece. It's important that you keep track of insights and ideas in a way that is easy to use and meaningful to you and your parenting team.

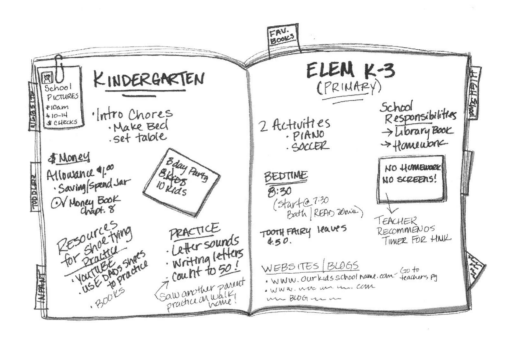

Write down the ideas, tips, goals, and advice that you want to use and remember.

Parents are so busy and easily distracted. If you find a great tidbit to add to your Parenting Roadmap, but you do not have it handy, text it to yourself, screenshot it, grab a piece of paper and jot yourself a note. Then make sure you put it into the right section of your roadmap! Even if it means printing that text to yourself and taping it into your roadmap.

Then, your notes will be ready for when you need them in times like this . . .

. . . hmmm, all you will need to do is check your Parenting Roadmap!

You may be wondering: How should I take notes for this Parenting Roadmap? The answer is: whatever way is most comfortable for you. Do you like to use outlines, bullets, or quick phrases?

Any notetaking style will do; just keep it quick, useful, and handy.

A LESSON IN WRITING PLANS FROM TEACHERS

Teachers manage classrooms full of kids with diverse personalities and abilities. How do they do it? Planning!

They plan routines to keep classroom tasks running smoothly. They create discipline plans to mentor and guide behavior. They structure lessons with purpose and fun to enhance learning.

As a teacher, I used to imagine how I wanted my classroom to operate. I wrote out plans and set up the classroom environment to support them. The next step was to show the kids how to follow the routines and rules in the classroom. I would practice the routines with the kids several times before letting the kids take them over independently.

Teachers also look ahead at curriculum goals for upcoming units, and they plan with the end goals in mind. They figure out the important objectives, vocabulary, and concepts kids need to know at the end. Then they plan backward toward the introduction lessons presented in the beginning, making sure all bases are covered until they finish the unit.

When I taught school, I would spend time reflecting on how a lesson went. What worked well in the lessons? What did not work well? I would make notes to reuse the good parts and change the bad parts for the following year.

Planning books help teachers stay on track, hold students accountable, and are a reference of their daily teaching efforts. Plans give teachers confidence and are an efficient way to teach kids.

Their plan books are not always beautiful. They are full of cross-outs, scribbles, and paper-clipped reminders, but those plan books are a teacher's most valuable tool.

Authoring teacher plans sounds like authoring a Parenting Roadmap!

If teacher plan books are a valuable tool for managing classrooms full of kids, then how much more valuable can a Parenting Roadmap be for parents managing their families?

Parents, too, can create and author a plan and look ahead to upcoming parenting issues to prepare for. We can show our kids how to do things and practice with them until they can do them by themselves. We can reflect on what is working and what is not, to change and fix our plans for the better.

I hope you have already marked up pages and written notes. I know how busy you are, and procrastinating makes this Parenting Roadmap harder to start.

Keep it easy and work on it a little each day or week. Nobody is grading your roadmap, so there is no need to wait for a better time to make it perfect.

"Procrastination makes easy things hard and hard things harder."– Mason Cooley

Get set up. Get on the same page. It may take a little time and work, just like setting up a budget, planning for a vacation, or writing your weekly grocery list. Still, over time as you discuss, research, observe others, and take notes about what you think the best plan is for your Parenting Roadmap, you will see how it becomes a valuable tool for your family. It's just like dieting and exercise; the sooner you get started, the sooner you will see the benefits of using this tool.

Solutions for Noteworthy Parenting

At this point, the solutions you have discovered and documented are now in your notes and ready to use. It's your foundation for parenting. Maybe you have set goals for your family as well and started preparing to achieve those goals. Way to go!

You are on your way, but the process is ongoing as you add to your Parenting Roadmap over the years. Try to stay a stage or two ahead of your kids so you will always have notes to rely on.

UPDATING YOUR PARENTING ROADMAP

At times, your plans may need updating or tweaking. We try to plan the best we can, but the unexpected happens, and things change.

Maybe there will be an area of parenting that you didn't think you would need to plan for, and you will have to add to your notes.

Maybe there will be a few notes that change a bit with each kid.

Maybe technology or societal changes require you to take a different path with your notes.

Updating your plan happens when things change or new things come along that require you to tweak your plan. Examples of updates could be:

- New technology
- Changes in the family budget
- Adjusting a curfew for special occasions
- Changing responsibilities in the family
- Setting new goals
- Starting new traditions

CHORES

Chores were an area that we updated often. We always felt it was important for kids to learn responsibility for chores starting at a young age. The problem was that I have never been the

world's greatest housekeeper myself. If a friend called to meet up at the park with their kids, I would leave my chores in an instant to go meet up with them. I admit, I never set the perfect example for housekeeping in my home, but somehow, the chores always got done.

As for chores with the kids, I would come up with strategy after strategy to keep our house clean. I always loved this quote by Mary Poppins, "In every job that must be done, there is an element of fun. Find the fun and snap the job's a game."

I kept this quote in mind as I devised each new chore plan. I had high hopes as I implemented each one that it would be the magic key to success.

We tried to beat the clock to clean the house.

I assigned each kid tasks that would be done once a week and labeled them on the family calendar.

We tried family cleanup times on Saturday mornings with loud party music.

We tried drawing chores out of a jar.

We tried chores with assigned monetary amounts.

I would make color-coded charts, diagrams, and lists.

I even went so far one time as to try teaching a little Spanish along with the chores. I called the new system "abierto la puerta." Sesame Street was on in the background for the younger kids, talking about the word abierto, which is Spanish for "open." I remembered that "door" was la puerta from my Spanish 101 class. I put the two together to create this very clever, so I thought, little chores plan. The plan was simple. We could not do activities each morning until our chores were done and we could open the door to the world and invite guests to come in. This plan only lasted a few weeks, but at least the kids learned a bit of Spanish, right?

I tried to make doing chores as fun as possible. Unfortunately, the part I was weak in was consistency and follow-up when the kids began to fall off the wagon. They fell off the wagon because I fell off the wagon.

I never gave up, though! While it was a disjointed example of how to do chores, they all learned to do their own laundry, dishes, cooking, vacuuming, mopping, and cleaning toilets. Yes, occasionally, we had our share of pink underwear and sweaters that shrunk to fit a Barbie doll, but I chalk those up to learning experiences. Learning experiences that taught my kids about chores better than any lecture or chart I could have created.

They all learned to pitch in and help. All I had to do was give them lead time and a plan, and they all showed up ready to clean.

Well, that sums up the IDEAS process. In the next chapter, we will follow a family through the process as they work to set a bedtime routine for their family.

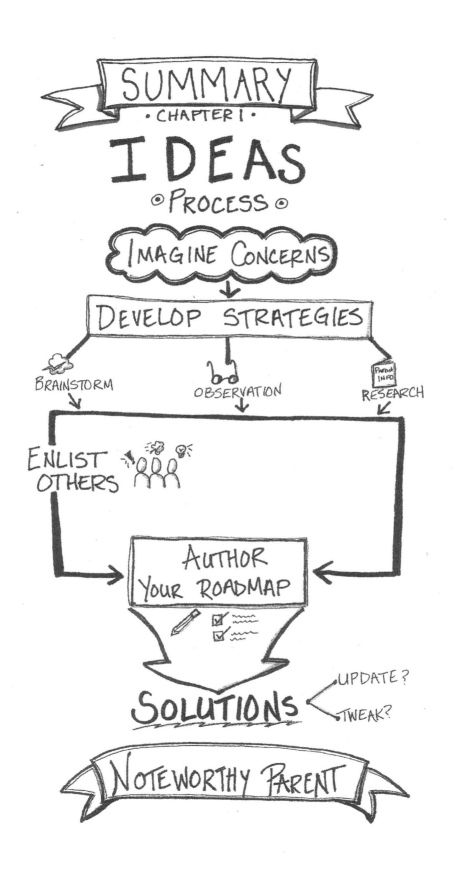

CHAPTER 2

IDEAS in Action: Bedtime Routine

"Discontent is the first necessity of progress."
— Thomas A. Edison

It's nine o'clock at night. You deny the third request for a drink of water and the final plea for one more story. Sigh! Why is bedtime so painful every night?

You are beyond discontent with the state of the family bedtime routine. Therein lies your first step toward making progress and fixing this common parental annoyance.

Nailing down a bedtime routine that tackles all of the tasks, settles down the kids, and is done by a set time every night is a challenge for most families. In this chapter, we will use this issue to walk through the IDEAS process with Parent A and Parent B. You will be able to see how the process works with one topic from beginning to end.

IMAGINE CONCERNS

Parent A and Parent B have a toddler and have just begun their Parenting Roadmap. Each one imagined concerns that they would like to sort out. In the sketch, they both want to fix the bedtime routine, so that is where they will begin.

DEVELOP STRATEGIES

Next, Parents A and B will need to develop strategies. As a part of this step, parents can brainstorm, observe, and research in order to find strategies that will fit their parenting styles. Parents A and B are overachievers and do all three for us to see.

BRAINSTORMING

These parents brainstormed creative solutions. Now they need to select the best one or two options so they can get started.

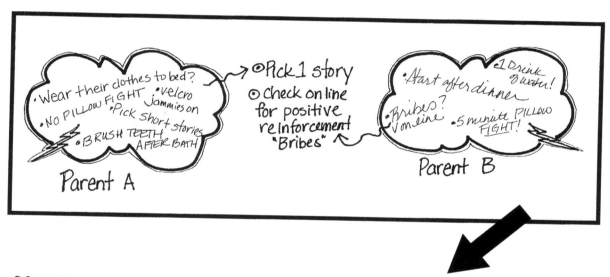

OBSERVING

Ever observed a great parenting moment and thought to yourself, I need to try that? Parent B observed a friend using a sticker chart to encourage her kids to take naps. Parent B immediately texted Parent A to discuss using a sticker chart for the bedtime routine. Parent A is exhausted and eager to add this as a potential strategy on their Parenting Roadmap.

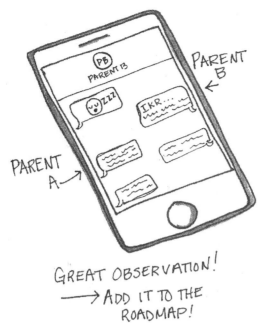

GREAT OBSERVATION!
→ ADD IT TO THE
ROADMAP!

RESEARCHING

Parents A and B are now researching their strategies. In the pictures, we see they have not only marked a few good spots in a book on bedtime routines, but they're looking into a class on the subject, and they also found online resources.

The next step is to write down the best notes from these references to discuss what strategy they will use for their Parenting Roadmap.

Keep track of where you found your notes in case you need to refer back to a particular chapter in a book or website.

ENLIST OTHERS

Now let's look at how parents A and B might enlist others for help. Share your concerns with the parents in your network. Chances are, someone has experienced a similar problem, and they may have strategies to share.

AUTHOR YOUR ROADMAP

Parents A and B have been busy keeping track of their strategies for the bedtime routine scenario. Here are several different examples of how they may decide to write their notes for their Parenting Roadmap:

Bedtime Routine Table

Time	Activity	Completed/Notes
7:30 – 8:00	Bath/teeth/potty	
8:00 – 8:15	Dirty clothes Prep tomorrow clothes	
8:15 – 8:30	Story/check-in/XOXO	

Bedtime Routine Checklist

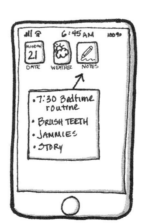

Bedtime
1. Bath/ brushteeth
2. Jammies
3. Story/kiss

- [ ] Bath/jammies
- [ ] Bush teeth
- [ ] Go potty
- [ ] Put dirty clothes in basket
- [ ] Layout tomorrows clothes
- [ ] Check in/talk
- [ ] Read story
- [ ] Kiss goodnight

SOLUTIONS FOR NOTEWORTHY PARENTING

Parent A and Parent B needed to update their solutions make sure they added extra time to go over and reinforce the sticker chart, so they tweaked their original plan, as you can see.

Bedtime Routine Table

Time	Activity	Completed/Notes
7:30 – 8:00	Bath/teeth/potty	
8:00 – 8:15	Dirty clothes Prep tomorrows clothes	
8:15 – 8:30	Story/check-in/XOXO	

Insert updates as needed...

Review sticker chart

You can now see how the process looks with one scenario all the way through. Maybe you also found a helpful takeaway for your family bedtime routine.

SLEEP SAVER KIT

You are in a deep sleep when suddenly you feel a little tap on your shoulder. You turn your head on your pillow to find one of your kids two inches from your face, staring at you. You are groggy but manage to ask them why they are up. Here is where any number of reasons can be inserted into this situation.

I had a nightmare.

Thunder and lightning woke me up.

Why hasn't the tooth fairy come yet?

The three words I hated to hear the most were: I threw up. This meant leaving the covers and going from groggy to game on. Those three words meant new pajamas, new sheets, and more vomit was coming.

There was a period of time in our house when our kids shared rooms. The two girls in one room, and the two boys in the other, all on bunk beds.

The bunk beds were made with iron bars supporting the mattresses and iron bars for the ladder rungs. Often, the mattresses would push against the wall, leaving some space to see below between the rungs.

I'm explaining the design of the bunk beds because one night, I got a tap on the shoulder from one of the top bunkers on the bed. They woke up and got sick with no chance of getting down the ladder, which was hard on their feet to begin with.

As I headed down the hall, the smell foreshadowed the disaster ahead. I stood in the doorway, stunned by the sight.

The younger child in the lower bunk bed was still sleeping and had been narrowly missed by the downward flow of vomit between the open rungs from the top bunk. Then I noticed that vomit had made it through the rungs of the bottom bunk into the under dresser, filled with clean, folded clothes. Even the carpet was hit.

As a parent, you are allowed to spend a moment in shock before pulling yourself together. I did.

Where do you start?

How do you avoid the vomit in order to remove the still-sleeping child?

Are you starting to feel nauseous from the odor and sight of it all?

Then it's time to roll up your pajama sleeves and dive in. Clean up the sick kid and get them a bucket and a new makeshift bed set up somewhere near a bathroom.

Access the clean kid and move them to a sleeping bag in the other sibling's room and away from the sick kid.

Clean up as much as you can, start a load of laundry, and spend the rest of the night dozing in-between throw-ups from the sick kid, who will need your help and sympathy.

This is rough. You can, however, minimize the impact of these middle-of-the-night wake-up calls by creating a sleep-saver kit.

Think of all the reasons you could be awakened and collect all the gear you will need. You can store these items in a bin that goes under your bed or in an empty drawer or cupboard.

So, what items work well?

- Thermometer
- Kids Tylenol and Advil
- Your doctor's after-hours care number and your healthcare information
- A bucket or container for throwing up
- Sanitizing wipes
- A stash of money for the tooth fairy
- Nightlight or little flashlight

- A few books
- An extra pillow and a blanket or two

Now when you get the little tap on the shoulder, you won't have to hunt for a thermometer, or a book for them to quietly look at in your room after a thunderstorm. You can use the extra blanket and pillow to make them a little bed on the floor if needed.

You are prepared to help your kids as quickly as possible, so everyone can get back to sleep!

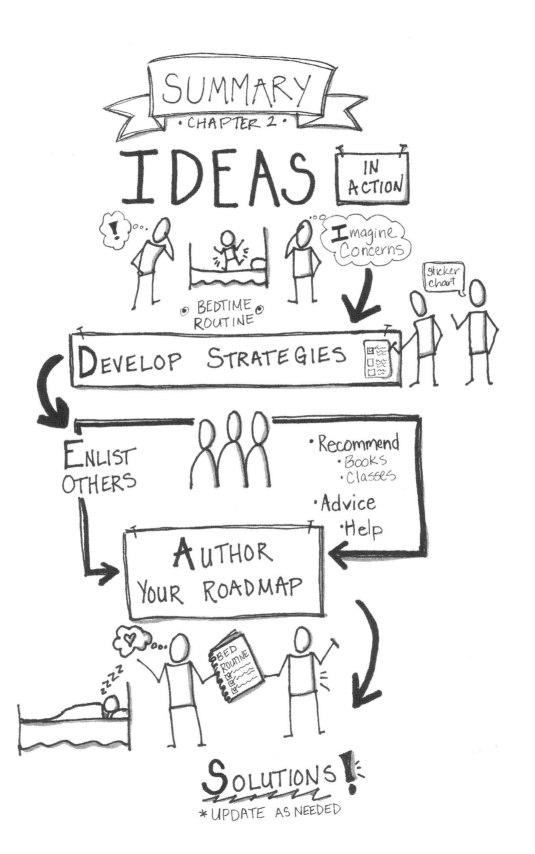

CHAPTER 3

The 3 Gears of Parenting

"My mission in life is not merely to survive, but to thrive; and to do so with some passion, some compassion, some humor and some style."
— Maya Angelou

When my husband and I started parenting, our strategy was survival.

After constructing a roadmap with a bit of passion and compassion, we felt like we were thriving as a family, with a healthy dose of humor and, we hoped, a bit of style.

The 3 Gears of Parenting seem to fall under these categories:

- Family bonding
- Coaching behaviors
- Letting go

These gears interlock to push parents along the journey of raising their kids, and offer deeper insights for your Parenting Roadmap.

FAMILY BONDING

The smell of Dad's Saturday morning pancakes, the competitive atmosphere during family game night, and hearing the crazy character voices Mom does during the bedtime stories all tie into the family bonding experience.

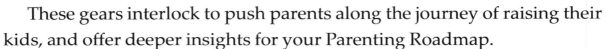

Family bonding weaves the people in the family together. The ties are routine, familiar, and cherished.

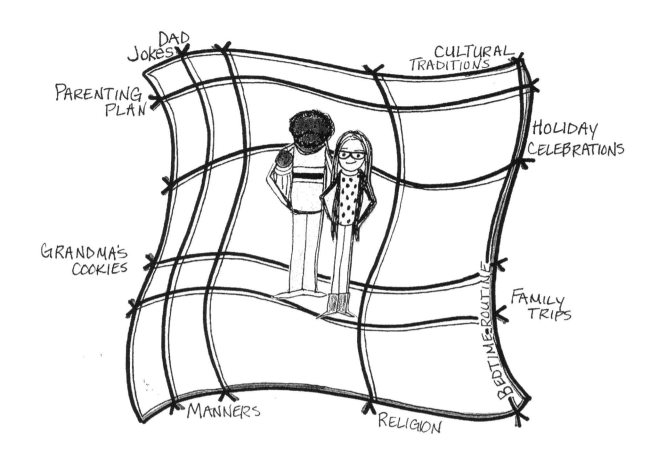

They are experiences unique to your family. Sure, you may have customs and traditions that are similar to other families, friends, or neighbors, but the details in which you come together as parents give your household a unique bond. Think of the favorite books you read at bedtime, holiday customs you intertwined from each parent's childhood, and a unique way you prepare a family recipe.

Whether your bonding experiences are daily habits or big seasonal holiday rituals, they are common connections for your family.

The bonds you create help your kids relate to other generations and people in the community. Through these activities, kids are learning respect, responsibility, trust, love, and a sense of belonging.

 What routines, traditions, and customs would you like to share with your children?

PILLOW PEN PALS

What started out as a way to help my kids practice reading and writing turned into a cherished bonding experience.

I purchased a fat mini-spiral notebook for each kid as they started kindergarten. I wrote a simple note or drew a picture in it and left it on their pillow with a pen attached.

Oh! The excitement over this little notebook! I explained to the kids that it was then their turn to write or draw a picture back to me and leave it on my pillow. We dated each entry and passed the notebook back and forth, using the pillows as mailboxes.

It was a fun early reading and writing activity, but it turned into so much more than that.

The kids would write to me about anything, including:

- A bully at school
- Grief over a lost loved one
- Excitement over an upcoming vacation
- Struggles
- Celebrations
- Simple "I love you, Mom" notes

I would, in turn, write back with:

- Ideas for help
- Encouragement
- Excitement
- "I love you back" messages

There were gaps in our writings as life got busy, or the notebook got lost under someone's bed. Once it was found again, the kids would pick up where we left off.

Occasionally, we would look back and notice how the kids' writing and drawing skills improved and how problems ended up getting resolved. We would reminisce about past trips, celebrations, or special notes.

It was a fun way to bond, mentor, and reinforce our values. It was like leaving little traces of our relationship throughout the notebooks.

The kids also asked about things that they may not have been comfortable talking about face-to-face, like what does a certain swear word mean, or admitting that they did something bad.

Over time, those little notebooks strengthened our bond with each kid. They each had their own book and enjoyed the system we had of writing back and forth.

It was a good heads up for parenting topics to plan for. When kids asked difficult questions or needed advice, it gave us as parents a little time to discuss a situation before responding.

Bonding with younger kids is pretty easy to do, but as time goes on and kids get older, parents begin to dread the rebellious, eye-rolling, pouting teenager stage. Our children's bodies are changing, hormones are affecting their emotions, and they are trying to fit in with friends.

One minute, teens want more freedom and space, and the next, they are clinging for emotional support. One minute they are having a nice conversation, and the next they are quiet and uninterested. While this is normal, there are a few ways that you can work to connect during these years.

Over the course of my parenting career, I happened upon a few good teen bonding activities. Most of them were by chance, and here they are:

- Leave out an old family video or photo album on the coffee table for them to come across.

- Dinner and a movie.

- Watch a favorite vintage TV show.

- Do a race or fundraiser together.

- Volunteer in the community.

- Try bucket list items like parasailing, roller coasters, or backpacking.

- Put them in charge of planning a family outing that they are interested in . . . The theater? A concert? Restaurant reservations? A sporting event? Putt-putt? Tours?

CLEANING THE BASEMENT WITH THOSE TEENAGERS

Our unfinished basement had become overloaded with boxes full of the kids' school papers, mementos, and general pack rat types of items that they had each collected over the years. It was time to go through it as some of my kids were getting ready to move out of the house, and the other two were teenagers.

The kids needed to condense, donate, or throw out what they no longer wanted. The rest needed to be packed up to take with them.

I gave them a heads up a few weeks before, so they were prepared to do this dreaded project.

As the first few items came out, however, the journey down memory lane began.

Look at how I used to draw.

It's my kindergarten Halloween costume!

Look at these baby blankets!

My rainbow teddy bear!

Here's the Cinderella nightgown I wore in preschool . . . torn, shredded, and well-loved!

Check out my old keychain collection . . . (twenty minutes passes here as everyone reminisces about each keychain)

What should've taken an hour to sort turned into a whole day's project. We had fun. We laughed. We got a bit sentimental.

So, save some school papers, old favorite T-shirts, stuffed animals, artwork, and mementos from the early years so you can go through them later during a rough patch with your teenagers.

The family-bonded relationship you create begins to interlock now with the next gear, which is coaching behaviors. You are creating a reliable and predictable environment so that you can now mentor your child(ren).

COACHING BEHAVIORS

While kids are busy learning, making mistakes, and experimenting with the world around them, they are not always thinking of the safety, boundaries, or impacts of their actions. They are impulsive, curious, self-centered, and well, sometimes mischievous.

They need reminders, consequences, and a lot of coaching to stay safe and learn how to interact in the world around them. They need help with learning to stop and think, manage emotions, think of others, and make good choices.

You will be thrown more curveballs seen as pouts, fits, rebellions, and bad choices than you would like to over your parenting career. By thinking and planning ahead, you can teach and mentor ahead of the curve. This will not eliminate every meltdown, but like teaching kids to do chores or save money, you can teach them about behaviors and give them a head start on learning to manage their actions.

Kids struggle to overcome the emotions of the moment. Those emotions drive the impulsive, instant gratification, brewing frustration, and heated anger episodes that kids need help learning how to manage.

EXPECTATIONS

Talking with kids ahead of time about behavior, routines, and expectations, as well as managing behavior, is a great place to start. Then when an issue begins to brew, you can remind them of the strategies you have previously presented. It may take a few or sometimes several episodes for kids to have the self-control to use the strategies, but stick with it.

Once kids' emotions blow up, the time for mentoring and coaching is gone until things cool off. At this point, it's key to remove them from a situation until they calm down. Once they have cooled off, the brain is ready for talking.

Keep the talking simple. Let the kids talk about how things went down and let them suggest how they could react better next time. This teaches them to reflect and learn to develop ideas and strategies on their own. Over time, it will help them learn to make better choices and manage the impulse of the moment.

Stick to your plan and reduce the number of behaviors you will have to endure.

Subconsciously, kids know the boundaries are good. They feel secure in having clear routines and rules set up. They want them. We know this because kids love to impose rules and justice on others, and they want the rules to be the same for others as they are for themselves. They lack the maturity to manage all the impulsive behavior roadblocks. With practice and time, they will get it.

As parents, we also need to prepare for kids to push back against the system.

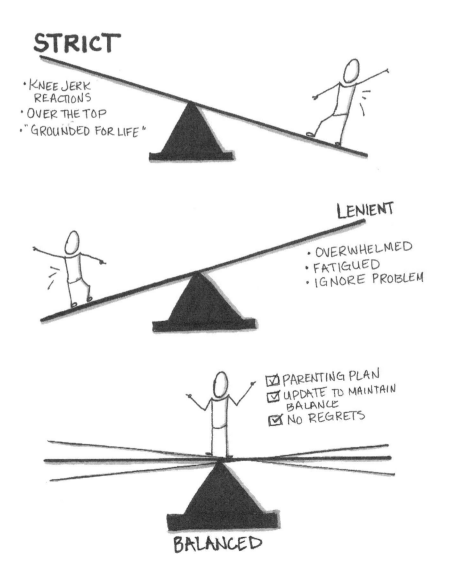

TEAMWORK

Being "on the same page" is what we hear in team sports or business organizations, and it is just as important to families. Taking the time to plan your discipline as a team is a critical piece of your Parenting Roadmap. Parents should create and agree on the rules and consequences, which presents a balanced approach.

When you take the time to plan, you avoid the "deer in the headlights" feeling when an issue comes up. You save time and can move to execute the plan. When parents are on the same page with discipline, they are confident, and the boundaries are clear to the whole family.

Imagine a business without a plan. If employees offered customers different prices and delivery dates, or treated some customers better than others, customers would not know what to expect each time they visit. Customers would be angry and irritable.

Families need rules, boundaries, and expectations for all to follow.

Kids will need a lot of practice with the rules and expectations, but the clearer you make the path for them, the easier it will be for both the kids and the parents to stick to the roadmap.

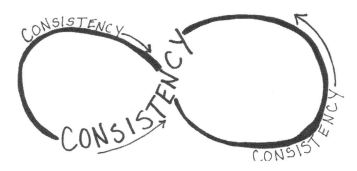

Consistency! Consistency! Consistency! Being consistent is as important as being on the same page. Kids will test the boundaries and try to get their way over and over again, but the quicker you redirect them back to the path, the quicker they will wear down, and the quicker it will become a habit to stay on the path.

PLAN AHEAD

Parents with no roadmap decide the rules in the heat of the moment or fly by the seat of their pants. They often make rash decisions, are likely to change the rules, or forget the rules they set in the first place.

Since the rules were created "on the fly" or "in the heat of the moment," the parents lack confidence and get worn down. In these instances, parents may forget the rules, begin to make exceptions to the rules, or over-react.

It's anarchy, and kids instinctively take full advantage of this situation. Truly, wouldn't we all?

This inconsistency shows kids loopholes, which then turn into exhausting and endless circles of behavior management for parents. It makes the job of behavior management harder as time goes on because the kids learn how to manipulate the lack of a system. Manipulation includes statements such as:

- But last time you said I could . . .
- (Dad or Mom) said it was okay already . . .
- You let (sibling's name) go; why can't I?
- Whine . . . moan . . . whimper . . . whine . . . moan. Sooner or later, the parents give in!
- (Insert friend's name)'s parents let them (insert activity); why don't you let me?
- It's not fair that I am grounded for two days. Last time it was only one . . .

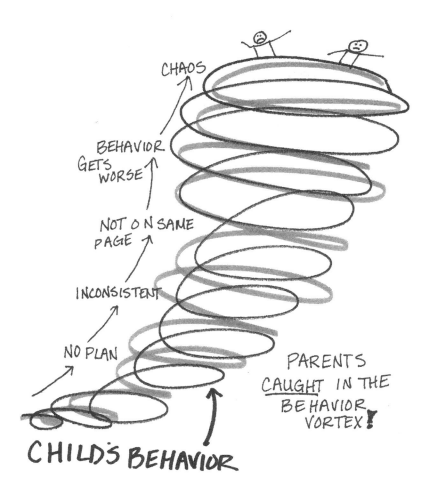

CHAOS

BEHAVIOR
GETS
WORSE

NOT ON SAME
PAGE

INCONSISTENT

NO PLAN

PARENTS
CAUGHT IN THE
BEHAVIOR
VORTEX!

CHILD'S BEHAVIOR

I learned, as a parent and a teacher, that while it is in our nature to think that we only need to communicate rules one time and kids should understand and follow them right away, we become annoyed when they don't, and really annoyed when they don't over and over again.

Some kids will need a lot of reminders, and others will not, but always be prepared for the long haul instead of the shortcut. That way, if it turns out to be easier, then woohoo! If, however, it is a real grind, you will be ready and hunkered down for the repeat button of the rules.

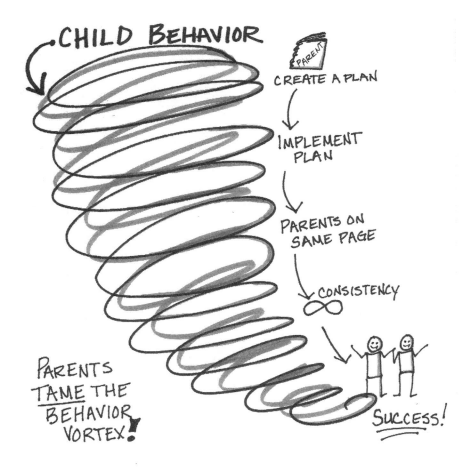

CHILD BEHAVIOR

CREATE A PLAN

IMPLEMENT PLAN

PARENTS ON SAME PAGE

CONSISTENCY

PARENTS TAME THE BEHAVIOR VORTEX!

SUCCESS!

Prepare for the worst, and that will help you gain the perspective and stamina needed to carry on.

Need strategies to ponder to get you started?

COACHING STRATEGIES

Give kids a heads up. It allows them to finish what they are doing or prepare for what is coming. You can say, In 10 minutes, it will be time to clean up your toys, or we will leave in five minutes; be ready to grab your coat. Another opportunity to give a heads up is when kids will need to start taking over a responsibility like paying for their own car insurance, entertainment, or rent.

Let the punishment fit the crime (sometimes called "natural conse-quences") is another approach parents can use. An example of this is when your child refuses to wear a coat on a cold day. You let them leave without the coat, and they freeze and regret not wearing it. Lesson learned — well, usually. Some kids can be tough to crack, and you have to let go of people thinking you are a bad parent for allowing your kids leave without a coat, but this one saves a lot of nagging.

Look the other way sometimes and give kids a little time before jumping into a situation. See if they can resolve a problem on their own. For instance, when kids are playing a game and arguing who will go first. You may feel an argument and maybe even violence brewing, but then, out of the blue, they decide to flip a coin — and you are off the hook as a referee!

Positive reinforcement is a feel-good strategy. Catch your kids doing good things and compliment them. Good behavior should be the norm, but when your kid goes above and beyond, notice it. It balances out all the things we see them do wrong.

Simple routines make life predictable and make kids feel secure. Routines for bedtime, homework, or cleaning offer kids opportunities to take respon-sibility, and eliminate the need to teach each step every time you want a task done.

Teaching manners is a good strategy to help kids learn to think of others and manage emotions. Being polite helps people get along in the world. Please, thank you, I'm sorry, and excuse me can help keep tempers at bay within the household and out in public.

Maybe add a little drama to your parenting when you mentor behav-iors. Using "the mom look" and body language allows you to get a point across quickly without words. Focused eye contact, or a subtle eyebrow raise with a tight-lipped mouth, gets a message across! It can either create a bit of a game for a repeated issue, or send a severe signal, depending on how much you emphasize your expression. This strategy can save you from over-nagging or yelling. Kids seem to move faster when the body language is strong, and no words are coming out. Pulling this off is a real parenting confidence boost and can add a bit of fun to your parenting.

Another silent strategy is the waiting game. Wait to reply to a request until kids fulfill their duties, such as homework or chores. You can even wait silently while looking at their unfinished homework to draw their attention to what needs to happen before you move on to their request. Surprised by a situation or behavior? Tell them you need to think about the consequence or talk with the other parent before you can let them know the consequence. For them, the waiting seems like a punishment.

Lastly, you may consider using charts and rewards to mentor and reinforce behaviors.

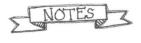 What will your expectations, boundaries, and routines be? What will your strategies and consequences be? How will they change as kids get older? What's your behavior management style?

Coaching behaviors can include character-building activities as well.

SHARING A BIRTHDAY PARTY

We began a birthday party tradition that took time to convince the kids of what a good idea it was.

The kids had one year that they could have a big party with lots of friends. Instead of gifts, though, they needed to collect items to donate to the local homeless shelter or the food bank. This special birthday party was held around the fifth- or sixth-grade year. The kids could choose which year they wanted to have it.

On the surface, they liked the idea. Under their breath, there was grumbling.

They would ask, Why can't we get a present AND ask for a donation? To which we replied that there were already too many toys and treasures in the house. Buying a gift and making a donation was a lot to ask of guests, too.

The invitation stated that in lieu of gifts, please bring a donation of one of the listed items. When many of the parents RSVP'd, they would ask if they should also bring a gift, but we told them their donation and the presence of their child was a perfect gift.

On the day of the party, kids showed up with the donations, which we stacked off to the side. Everyone played games, ate cake, and had a fun time.

When the parents came to pick up their kids, they were surprised to see how many donations there were. The kids were amazed too, and some ended up having donation parties of their own.

After all the guests were gone, we drove the donations to the homeless shelter and dropped them off.

That is when the magnitude of the party really hit the kids. They were overwhelmed with the difference they were able to make. Did they miss getting presents from their friends? They did not miss gifts at all in that moment.

I should mention that they still did get gifts from their grandparents and us, but it was a great lesson learned.

Our kids may not be able to tell you the details of all of their birthdays now, but they remember that birthday party fondly and vividly.

Having too many toys and things is a struggle for many families today. Kids need to learn the difference between wants and needs. They need to learn the value of money.

MONEY MANAGEMENT

While putting our Parenting Roadmap together, my husband and I decided that there were areas we would like to teach our kids about financial management. The flow of money is not endless, and kids need to learn that.

In middle school, we gave them a heads up that there were things they would need to get a job to pay for in high school. They would need money for their entertainment, gas, and some clothing purchases.

We talked to them in early high school about what they would be responsible for upon graduation. They would need to pay for car insurance, a car payment, and cell phone fees.

Part of turning eighteen and becoming an adult is taking responsibility for your finances, so we broke it down and gradually handed over the bills.

We gave them an early heads up and sprinkled a few reminders along the way. They were prepared when the time came to take over these financial responsibilities. Here's what we did to guide our kids with money management:

Opened savings and checking accounts with them early, to help them gradually understand how accounts work.

Purchased stocks as gifts, so they could monitor the stock and learn about investing. We tried to get stocks for companies they were interested in, like Disney.

When they wanted expensive items like a letter jacket, golf clubs, or prom dresses, we let the kids borrow the portion they would pay. We agreed on a system for paying us back, and we kept track of the loan in a little notebook. We tore out the loan page once it was paid off.

The kids needed to secure loans for college. My husband and I would put our saved amount toward their loans once they graduated.

As long as they were in college, they had free rent, groceries, and healthcare at home, but once they turned twenty-one, they were responsible for all their bills, eating out, and travel expenses.

Planning out each financial stage gave us time to mentor the kids little by little instead of in one big session as they were moving out.

 What character-building activities will you include in your Parenting Roadmap?

Here is where family bonding and coaching behaviors gradually turn into the Letting Go gear. Kids begin to do things for themselves and mature. Parents begin to let go bit by bit.

LETTING GO

This third gear of parenting is about going from doing everything for your child to accepting their complete independence into adulthood. It is a gradual process that starts in infancy, when your child is completely dependent on you.

Over the years, you teach, coach, and mentor them every step of the way by showing the tasks, then sharing the tasks, and finally letting go of the tasks altogether. It involves a little family bonding and coaching behaviors to accomplish this.

You do the task, then you practice it together. You give your best advice and tips, and they begin to catch on. Before you know it, they take over the tasks.

There will be mistakes, learning curves, backsliding, and reteaching, but eventually, the tasks move from your responsibility to theirs. Some of the great teachable moments of letting go happen during the elementary school years.

THE SCHOOL PROJECT

Oh! The last-minute school projects!

I'm talking about the kind of assignment that always involves at least one or two errands to get supplies, and then monitoring the late-night

construction into the wee hours. You help finish the masterpiece and go to bed with marker-colored fingers and glue in your hair. I even pulled this one a few times as a kid.

As a parent, you are usually informed the night before the big due date. It is typically the busiest night of the week, and you are now in a position to squeeze in more errands and homework time.

How could you change this scenario for the future? Your child used their planner to mark the assignment but blew off the work until the night before.

Moving forward, you need a better plan. How are you going to mentor them to spread out the assignment over time? How can you teach them to give you a heads up on the supplies they need earlier so you can pick up those items during your routine shopping trips?

Maybe you could post a calendar on the fridge for homework and projects or set up a check-in time for assignments on Saturday mornings while eating pancakes?

The elementary years are a great time to work with the teachers to teach kids responsibility. Teachers often have great behavior management plans in place for these very issues, and I feel that parents worry too much about how they or their kids will look to the teacher if things are not perfect.

As parents, we need to let go of trying to be perfect. Teachers, worth their weight in gold, are more interested in teaching kids life lessons right alongside the parents. Let your child deal with the consequences at school for a late assignment or a forgotten lunch. They may miss:

- Recess time to finish the homework they forgot
- Checking out a new book at the library until they return the one they forgot
- Lunch, but usually the cafeteria will give something to kids who forgot their lunch
- Full credit for that big project they pushed off

Of course, you might rescue a kindergartener more often, as they are still getting used to going to school, but each year, add more things to the list that you will not rescue them for.

It's easier to let kids fail when you have mentored them along and they are not catching on. You have stuck to your plan and you know it's time to let them learn by natural consequences.

When you don't have a parenting plan, you continue to try and keep your head above water and feel guilty that you have not taken the time to teach your kids time management. This results in you constantly rescuing them in order to put out the next parenting fire.

Both planning and not planning to teach responsibility will take your time.

"By failing to prepare, you are preparing to fail." – Benjamin Franklin

The goal is to lead your kids to complete the projects independently. If you implement a plan, you get to slowly pull yourself off of the responsibility as your child takes over.

If you don't plan, you may not be using time on the teaching process, but you will always be in a position to make that last-minute shopping trip and help throw together that science fair or book report project into the wee hours of the night.

The gradual letting go of responsibility and knowledge doesn't happen overnight. Nor are children ready for all-in-one sessions of the information and responsibilities they will need as adults.

Here is an example of how you can mentor your children over time to meal prep—a life skill all kids should learn.

Chore Evolution

SET TABLE → DISHES → COOK → BUY GROCERIES → HOST DINNER

You prepare their food when they're young, but as kids grow, they learn to grab or make a simple snack. Then you follow a recipe together, teaching them how to measure ingredients. As teenagers, they learn to use knives, hot pans, and hopefully, the dishwasher. Once they can drive, maybe they pick up items at the grocery store for you. When they move out, they can read a recipe, grocery shop, and cook for themselves. (If not, there is always take-out and delivery.)

Here are a few more responsibilities you can gradually teach over time. Kids can learn to:

- Make and pack lunches
- Complete homework and school projects independently
- Make their beds and pick up their rooms
- Learn to call and set up a haircut, doctor, or dentist appointment
- Mop, wash dishes, and clean a bathroom
- Sew and mend clothes
- Wrap gifts
- Address an envelope
- Use tools for simple home repairs
- Do yardwork
- Keep track of calendar events and learn time management skills
- Take care of auto upkeep, getting gas, oil changes, and flat tires

As you continue to mentor them into adulthood, consistency is another important factor in becoming successful in this area.

Many times they will forget or resist wanting to do the task you are trying to teach them. The reality is that it may take several times of showing and reminding them how to complete tasks. Consistency is the key to forward progress!

 I would like to recommend a great picture book for teaching initiative to kids. It is The Dog Poop Initiative by Kirk Weisler. Not only does the title get kids' attention, but it is a true story about a dog who poops on a soccer field. Some people point out the poop, some avoid the poop, until finally, somebody picks up the poop.

Teach kids to take action when they know something needs to be done. Don't wait for someone else to do it . . . do it!

If the alarm goes off, then get up and start getting ready for school.

Begin your homework without a reminder.

If snow has fallen, grab the shovel!

One of the most significant times of letting go of the kids is when they leave for college or get a job and move out. They may still need guidance as far as setting up student loans or signing rent agreements, but it's time for them to take responsibility.

If your student decides to go away to college, healthcare decisions, as well as university red tape, are common areas in which eighteen-year-olds are expected to make decisions. However, they may still be thinking Mom and Dad are doing this for them.

If your young adult is going off to college, parents are informed at orientation that you have no legal access to their grades or information. This is often an abrupt discovery for parents.

You can look at this situation in a few ways. Maybe you feel they are ready to handle all the responsibility and red tape because you have planned for this and mentored them to fill out government applications, and it is time to sink or swim. Maybe you think they can manage some of this, but you know important things could fall through the cracks, and they need more mentoring. Or lastly, you may be thinking, God help us all, they are not ready, and if I don't get access to their records, they will fail miserably and bring down the whole university with them.

Young adults are not always ready to keep track of their Free Application for Federal Student Aid (FAFSA), taxes, grades, red tape, moving out, and paperwork or files in general. They typically do understand how to spend money and have fun really well, though.

Health Insurance Portability and Accountability Act (HIPAA) authorization and educational records release forms are two examples of information you may need access to or have conversations with your eighteen-year-old about. Your student may need to give you some level of permission to see and access these records, or maybe they feel they have things covered.

Here are a few reasons that planning for FAFSA and HIPAA ahead of time is valuable:

- If your eighteen-year-old has a medical emergency, somebody needs to have the ability to make medical decisions if they are incapacitated.

- Prescription refills can be held up if there are insurance and HIPAA issues.

- There are important deadlines and minimum course requirements for FAFSA loans. Your student may have to start paying loans early if they don't pay attention and follow the rules.

Young college students are in one of the biggest transition times of their lives. They don't have a lot of experience dealing with bureaucracy, staying on hold with government agencies, or digging for account numbers and information. Again, some eighteen-year-olds may be fine managing on their own, but even those kids may need a helping hand. It's not the fun part of being an adult, and it requires grit and perseverance, and they need to learn how to do it.

How do you and your college student feel about you having access to their school records or government loan accounts?

Are you okay with paying thousands of dollars for their college education and finding out at the end of the semester that they have not gone to class, and flunked out?

Many parents have saved for years or are borrowing a lot of money for college, and like any investment, they have a right to know how their investment and their student are performing. What will your plan be?

If you have a student who is responsible, and you don't feel you need access to their grades, you can request the grades at the end of the semester in exchange for a check to pay for the next semester's expenses.

Maybe it's time to let things go and see how they do.

This age includes a lot of gray areas with decisions. Every parent will have a different comfort level with each kid.

Think about why certain topics are essential for them to know and understand. Be prepared for questions that your kids may have. You don't have to be prepared for every answer. You can let your kids know if you do not have an answer, but you will look into it and get back to them.

BECOMING A PARENT CONSULTANT

Once your kids are established on their own as adults, they will often be back to get advice on things like:

- Buying their first house

- Tax questions
- Insurance
- Retirement investing
- Parenting
- Fixing . . . well, just about anything!

Here is where you take on the role of a parent consultant. Your kids may ask for your advice or help, and you share your expertise or ideas. Your kids may or may not take your advice as they are old enough to figure things out, but they still like to have your opinion or thoughts to help them.

Sometimes it may be a topic they need a lot of consulting on, like home mortgages and how they work, while other times it may be what laundry detergent do you think is best? Either way, parents continue guiding and helping kids even when they become adults. The further into adulthood they get, the more the ideas and advice go both ways.

Keep the door open for when they solicit your input, and remember, unsolicited advice may be best kept to ourselves.

 What responsibilities would you like to start teaching your kids? How can you break down those tasks over time? Make notes on your Parenting Roadmap under the age sections, jotting down how you want to teach them to go to the next level on a task.

SUMMARY

THE 3 GEARS OF PARENTING

Interlocking together to push parents along the journey

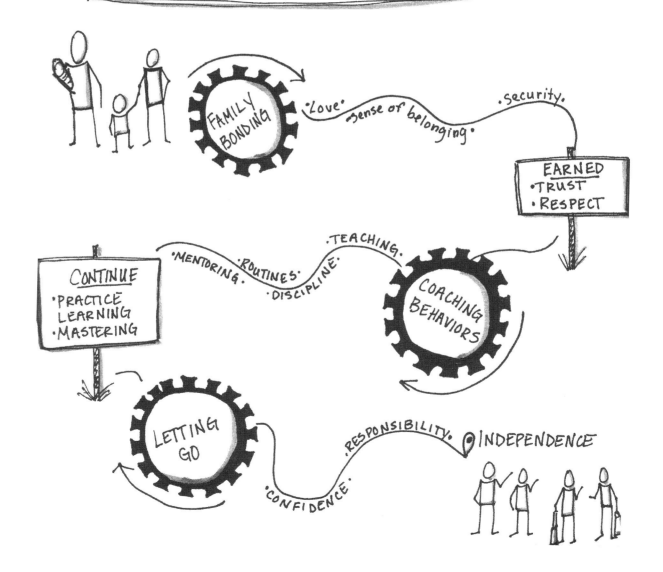

FAMILY BONDING

• Love • • Sense of belonging • • Security •

EARNED
• TRUST
• RESPECT

• TEACHING •
• MENTORING • • ROUTINES • • DISCIPLINE •

COACHING BEHAVIORS

CONTINUE
• PRACTICE
LEARNING
• MASTERING

LETTING GO

• RESPONSIBILITY • INDEPENDENCE
• CONFIDENCE •

CHAPTER 4

The Ever-Changing Technology Climate

"Technology is a great servant but a bad master."
— Adapted from Francis Bacon

The advancement of technology has improved many aspects of life. It helps us work efficiently, cure diseases, and connect globally.

This chapter will cover how technology affects families. We will look at the pace and magnitude with which technology is predicted to advance and how that leaves parents unable to look to the previous generation for guidance.

Follow the IDEAS process and create your own unique Parenting Roadmap for the technological advancements ahead.

THE SPEED OF TECHNOLOGICAL ADVANCEMENT

Remember studying the Industrial Revolution in school? The steam engine and the assembly line and how they advanced the efficiency of business, and our lives? That revolution took a lot of time and progressed at a rate that allowed people to digest the changes and adjust to them.

We live in an age where technology is moving at such a fast pace that innovations become obsolete, and new versions of technology are constantly in our midst. We have quickly moved to self-checkout lanes, iPad restaurant ordering, and the transfer of money via smartphone apps.

Companies are innovating and inventing new technology that will change our world at an increasingly faster rate each year. The World Intellectual Property Organization has seen the fastest growth of intellectual property rights applications for trademarks and patents over the past fifteen years.

"We stand on the brink of a technological revolution that will fundamentally alter the way we live, work and relate to one another in a scale and scope unlike anything humankind has experienced before." —Klaus Schwab

The learning curve for all of this is a part of almost every aspect of our lives, leaving little breathing room for parents to focus on, well, just parenting.

THE EFFECTS OF TECHNOLOGY THROUGH THE GENERATIONS

In the past century, each decade could brag about what it had to offer as industry and technology advanced us forward, but not many inventions can match the internet for its impact on the human race.

Not to head down the "back in the day we paid a nickel for a soda and didn't need video games for fun" bit, but you will probably hear a lot of that kind of talk from your older family members. Times may have been simpler generations ago, and older family members don't see the need for many of the advancements we have today—but technology is here to stay.

Our parents and grandparents think that most of these gadgets and smartphones are hogwash; however, they have found their way into the daily life of households today.

Just like when the lightbulb was invented and people moved from using candles and lanterns to light their houses, technology has become a part of everyone's households and a way of life for all of us today.

DATING

Dating is a topic that parents both fear and joke about. "My kids won't date until they're thirty-four!" It is one of the more significant milestones that you will need to plan for as a parent, especially now as teens are involved with different social media platforms and can check out various dating apps. The dating pool is so much bigger than it was in the past, and more hidden from adults.

- What important points do you want to share with your kids before they get ready to start dating?

- What are the new norms of dating and relationships for teens?

- What are dating safety issues to discuss with your teen?

- At what age do you feel comfortable letting your teens go on a date?

- What apps are they using to meet people?

- Will you want to meet the date?

- Will there be a curfew, or do you prefer to use an FBI-approved locator app?

Imagining what your concerns are and beginning to formulate a plan will not only prepare you but also your kids for this milestone as it approaches. You can talk ahead of time with your kids about your plan.

Similarly, the technology advancements of today will become a way of life for our children and their future households.

As parents, we must engage in the new world of technology and model the use of it. For example, technology allows parents to work from home, but we have a duty to model work-life balance. We have a duty to model putting the phone aside at the dinner table or limiting our time on social media.

PARENTS MAKE A DIFFERENCE

Parents, you are today's decision-makers! You are raising the next generation, and your decisions about technology will have a lasting impact on generations to come.

As technology is re-creating how we interact with others and the world around us, parenting best practices are rapidly changing. If we rely on outdated parenting practices, we limit our potential to prepare our kids for their future.

"There has never been a time of greater promise, or one of greater peril. Today's decision makers, however, are too often trapped in the traditional, linear thinking, or too absorbed by the multiple crises demanding their attention, to think strategically about the forces of disruption and innovation shaping our future. In the end, it all comes down to people and values. We need to shape a future that works for all of us by putting people first and empowering them." – Klaus Schwab

This quote speaks directly to the mission of this book. Parents must invent new methods to manage technology and not allow themselves to get overwhelmed or lost in the chaos of everyday life.

Where is the balance for the use of technology in your family? There is a lot of talk about screen-free time for kids. Does this mean kids should have no screen time at all? No. There are great educational programs and apps for kids on computers. There are great TV shows and movies that are entertaining. Technology is not bad.

How we use technology is what matters. How we teach our kids to use technology is what matters.

Take time to think about how your parenting approach to technology affects your children and your values.

SOCIAL MEDIA "SHARENTING"

One example of how technology has caught parents off guard is in the sharing of their kids' milestones and photos on social media.

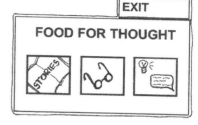

I did not even think of this aspect of parenting until I read the Wall Street Journal article by Joanna Stern, "Why I Put My Dog's Photo on Social Media, but Not My Son's." She talks about the safety factors of having your child's photo posted on public accounts.

She also talks about how parents have inadvertently shared embarrassing posts and photos of their little kids. Parents think every moment of their precious child is adorable, and it's fun to share those moments. They are not thinking at the time that twelve years later, their kids are going to be shocked and embarrassed when they see their potty photos on their parents' social media accounts. Once the kids grow up, however, and connect to their parents, they and their friends can see these old

posts. No person, let alone a teenager, wants pictures posted on the internet of themselves on the potty or doing something silly.

Those photos and posts are typically shared without much thought about the future.

How does this situation affect the way you will mentor your kids as they start their own social media accounts?

Will the tables turn as they catch your backside while you're cooking dinner, or maybe they'll post that old '80s photo of you on your birthday? Interesting points to ponder as you are creating your Parenting Roadmap.

Technological advancements are inevitable, and it is important to be aware of how they can affect the norms, ethics, and values of generations to come. You have the power to steer the direction of this global technological revolution for the betterment of your family and humanity.

How are you making this a priority?

What resources do you use to stay current with technological trends and policies?

How do you empower your kids to be successful and responsible users of technology?

How do you teach your kids to become good global citizens and possibly future parents?

How can you support the responsible advancement of technology in your community?

Vote and make your voice heard!

Like other topics in this book, there are no specific right or wrong answers. Families will have different priorities, rules, and plans that they establish for technology use.

Having your ideas and plans laid out will prepare your strong foundation as you move through the technological advancements ahead.

USE THE IDEAS PROCESS TO MANAGE THE TECHNOLOGY STORM

What are the technology issues that you are imagining are on the horizon for your parenting? Start developing your strategies by researching, observing others, and brainstorming. Enlist other parents from your parenting network to divide and conquer all of the technology topics. Write down your solutions and strategies in the appropriate age sections of your Parenting Roadmap. Use your solutions as needed and be sure to update or tweak as needed.

Unlike the Bedtime Routine scenario earlier, where we followed one topic through the IDEAS process, this section will show different technology issues in each step of the "IDEAS" process. This will give you a broader look at the many technology topics parents face.

IMAGINE CONCERNS — TECHNOLOGY

Technology advancements provide a lot of opportunities for parents to imagine concerns. What is the right amount of technology for your family? How much time is okay to be logged on or plugged in? How will you set a good example for your kids with screen time? How will you stay ahead of new technological advances?

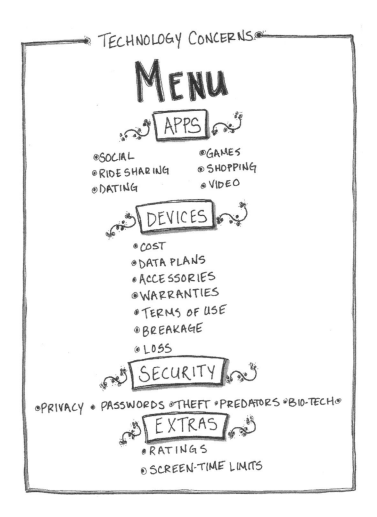

DRIVERLESS CARS

A great example of looking ahead may be to check out what is happening with the future of driverless cars. We hear a lot about it in the news as of the writing of this book, but it is still somewhat in experimental stages.

What would that look like for families and kids down the road? Maybe parents will be off the hook for teaching their kids how to drive, and that could save parents a lot of anxiety in the future.

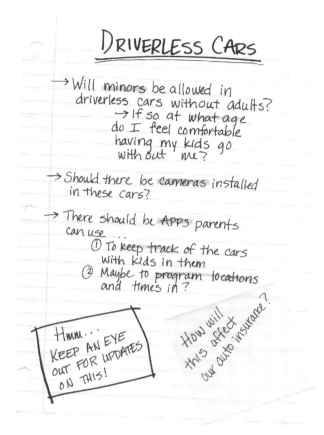

I'm sure there will be new parenting scenarios that go along with this new convenient technology. As you can see with this futuristic topic, you have many issues to ponder for your parenting notes. Leave blank space on your roadmap to update this one!

DEVELOP STRATEGIES — TECHNOLOGY

Brainstorming, observing, and researching help us to think through and find the best strategies and tools for managing all of the technology our families use.

This is a part of the process in which you will have to seek new ideas for your Parenting Roadmap. The generations before did not have to parent the new inventions of today.

MIA EARBUDS AND CHARGERS

If I had a nickel for every lost charger or set of earbuds in our house, I'd be a millionaire. The kids constantly misplaced these items. When they couldn't find their own, they would hijack somebody else's, claiming it was theirs.

You can imagine the heated arguments and accusations we endured. It was annoying to everyone in the house. No matter how well I hid my own, the kids could sniff them out like bloodhounds, and "borrow" them.

It was hard to nail down who took whose earbuds as they were all identical. It was a circle of parenting torture, and I could never catch anyone to make them purchase their own replacements.

Where do all these lost phone accessories end up, anyway?

We needed to brainstorm solutions. Did we need fingerprint kits? Lie detectors? Maybe implement an earbud tax on allowances?

Finally, we decided to purchase a rainbow assortment of permanent markers to color a portion of the cords. Each family member had their own color. Finally, peace of mind. If someone lost or destroyed their earbuds, they had to replace them on their own.

For other accessories and paperwork, prepare bins and create files to manage parts, directions, and warranties as needed. Not only will it save you time, but it will save a lot of unnecessary aggravation when the family is anxiously awaiting the use of the new device.

As new technology crosses your path, observe how others are managing the chaos, research ideas online, or invent your new strategies and systems.

ENLIST OTHERS — TECHNOLOGY

As a parent, I felt like I needed a staff to help me keep track of technology.

Today, laptops, tablets, smartphones, drones, streaming, watches, video games, Bluetooth, Alexa, and many other items not listed here are more parental management than just the TV remote of yesteryear.

Managing all of this is a monumental task. By the time you have researched, purchased, and set up new devices, you have only just begun.

ESTABLISH YOUR TECH TEAM

Here is a great example of one way you can enlist others and use your parenting network to divide and conquer the technology issues.

Most people are not experts in every aspect of parenting technology. Some parents are great at the setup and day-to-day updates needed, while others are experts at organizing the cords and paperwork, still others are great at talking with kids about how to safely search and share information online.

Get a group of parents together to share in the research and the work. Each parent can take part. Decide who is in charge of:

- New technology
- Upgrades

- Password formulas
- Pricing
- Parental protection software
- Organizing ideas for all the gear/paperwork and warranties
- Staying current on what is coming in the future

Then rely on each other's expertise. Everybody does not need to be an expert in every aspect of the home technology parenting issue. Share the work, and that gives you more time to enjoy parenting your kids.

Set up a social media group or a group email so you can all keep each other informed. Print, copy, or save what you need personally from this group for your roadmap.

A little teamwork can help each family to stay on top of the ethical and transformative issues of technology. The more parents work together, the more you can accomplish.

Your kids are watching! When they become parents someday, they will need to solve new technology issues we cannot even imagine yet, but they will be able to look to the tools of collaboration you used as a parent and plan for their Parenting Roadmap!

 What plans are you starting to formulate around technology?

AUTHOR YOUR ROADMAP — TECHNOLOGY

Part of authoring your Parenting Roadmap is to keep track of any resources you come across so you can use and revisit them as needed. Having trusted technology resources at your fingertips can help you stay current on the issues that will affect your Parenting Roadmap.

The parents' homepage on The Center on Media and Child Health website, cmch.tv, has a wide range of topics to search, even those set up by age. It's a great resource as you create your Parenting Roadmap for technology. The founder, Dr. Michael Rich, MD, MPH, an Associate Professor of Pediatrics at Harvard Medical School, Associate Professor of Social and Behavioral Sciences at the Harvard School of Public Health, and practicing physician in Adolescent Medicine at Boston Children's Hospital, has set up an excellent resource for parents looking to navigate media and technology for their families.

Want movie, TV show, video game, and book reviews for family content? Pluggedin.com or Commonsense-media.org are both great sites for parents. They give specific information about content so parents can make informed decisions about the media their kids are exposed to.

SOLUTIONS FOR NOTEWORTHY PARENTING — TECHNOLOGY

Having a solid plan in place gives you the confidence to share technology with your kids at a pace that is comfortable for you. This part of your Parenting Roadmap will probably need the most updating and tweaking. Technology advances quickly, and parents need to stay current on these trends.

With each new technological advancement, you become a parenting pioneer. You will create the norms of how to manage that technology, and set the bar for your parenting network.

You will bridge the gap between the technology of the generation before you while setting an example for the norms of parenting technology in future generations.

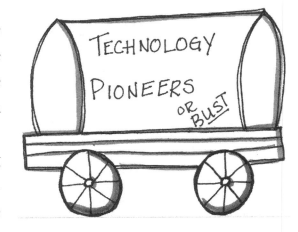

During our high school parenting career from the years 2006 to 2018, mobile phones evolved from simple cell phones used only for calls to smart-phones complete with internet and streaming capabilities.

Our parents never had to deal with parenting cell phones or constant upgrades. There was no cheat sheet for us; we had to invent our own norms. Our parents watched as we worked our way through this maze, developing new rules and systems and consequences with each new upgrade.

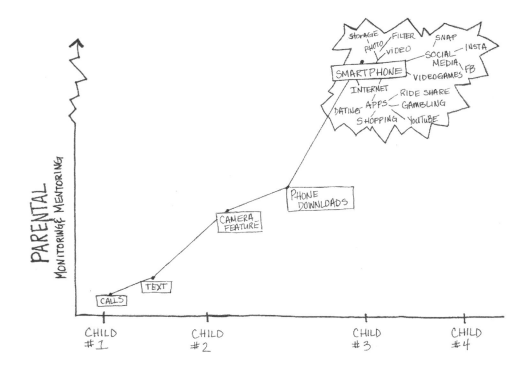

The upgrades came faster and were more powerful each time.

This required a lot of time learning the new features and attempting to predict the inevitable parenting issues that could follow. My husband and I would try out the new technology first. That gave us a chance to learn it and observe how other parents were managing the upgrades with their kids. Sure, our kids were always behind in the technology they used, but that plan worked out just right for us as parents.

In the future, your children will parent with even more new technology and challenges that we cannot predict! Thanks to you, however, they will understand the importance of thinking ahead and creating a roadmap to maximize their parenting skills.

 How will you stay updated on technology for your Parenting Roadmap? What technology concerns do you want to plan for?

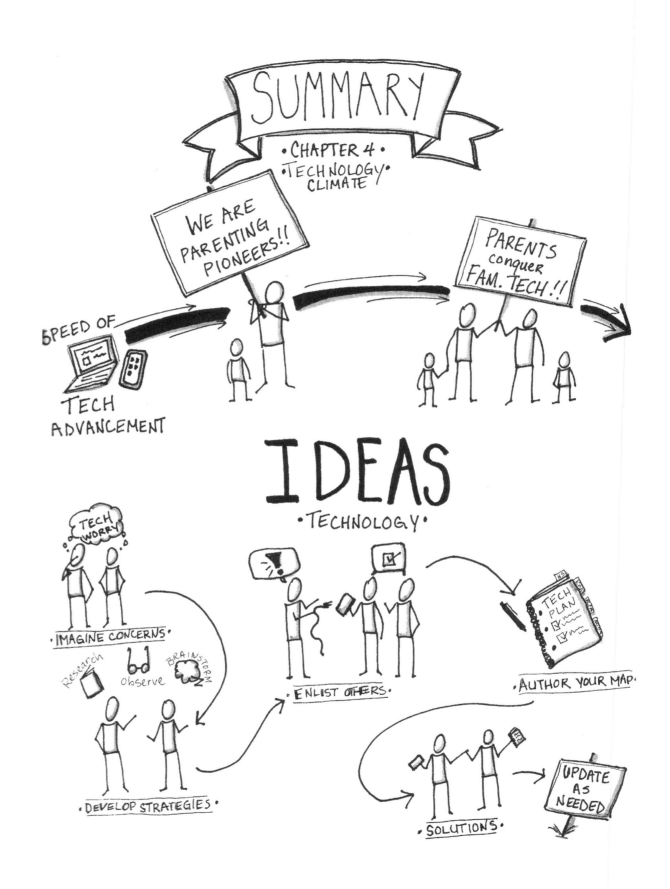

NOTES

CHAPTER 5

The Ever-Changing Social Climate

"(You) can't never let anything happen to him.
Then nothing would ever happen to him."
— Dory, *Finding Nemo*

New and changing issues in society constantly present themselves in front of families. Fewer filters exist in society today, which pushes parents to deal with topics before they feel their kids are ready and before they have pulled together a plan.

As parents, our instincts are to protect our children and to shelter them until they are older and more mature. We feel like Marlin, the overprotective clownfish dad in Finding Nemo. We know the dangerous issues and are scared about how to keep up with new, evolving ones.

Parents also want to expose their kids to their heritage, culture, or religion. This gives families and kids a sense of belonging and connection to a larger community. Kids learn how they are alike or different from others in society. It opens the door for kids to learn about other people while appreciating and sharing their backgrounds and traditions with others.

TOUGH TOPICS TO TALK ABOUT

Educating children on issues society presents is tricky. What are the appropriate ages to talk with kids about these topics? How can you begin talks before they learn about things online, or from others at school? What is the best way to introduce a topic, but wait to reveal more complex and adult parts of the talk for a later age? Do you feel ready to have talks about tough issues? How can you prepare mentally and emotionally to sit down and talk with your kids?

Start by staying current with what is happening in society, and following trends and new issues. The next step is to create a plan. Then create an atmosphere of trust, so your kids feel comfortable coming to you about topics that are hard for them to ask about.

Kids will hear about these issues at school, with friends, or possibly online, and that is even more reason to stay current and make sure you are educating and mentoring your children.

Create a plan that works for you and builds your parenting confidence.

It is a tough job. Take it one step at a time!

PARENTING IN THE MODERN SOCIAL ENVIRONMENT

Watching the news and reading reliable articles help parents keep an eye on trends in society that affect families. Consider both sides of issues by varying the news sources you use. Talk things over as parents. Write down your views and plans, then talk with your kids.

The Wall Street Journal is a great resource for parents and one I use daily. They regularly touch on technology, social issues, and parenting topics in the Life and Arts section.

Many topics may spark emotional or passionate feelings, and it is vital to take a deep breath and find a path that leads to best practices for raising the future generation.

They may be topics you are close to or those you do not know much about. Take the opportunity to learn more so you can be prepared to talk with your child.

Remember, technology has had a huge impact on the speed at which social change spreads. The internet provides kids with access to more and more information with a quick search. Parents must think about how this will fit into their plan.

What tools can help?

Which child protection software fits your needs?

How can you teach kids about searching safely online?

What are good strategies to share with kids about truthful versus untruthful sources on the internet?

What steps should kids take if they find inappropriate or hurtful things online?

Most social topics pop up in the pre-teen and teenage years, but by planning in advance, you will be able to lay a foundation with younger kids. This will help avoid giving one long lecture as these topics land in your lap.

Don't worry if your plan isn't perfect. Don't worry if you stumble a bit when talking with your kids. Don't worry if later you change your point of view!

Don't live **IN FEAR** live **INFORMED**

It is essential that you are doing your best to be a well-informed parent. You are doing your best to educate and prepare your kids. You are showing your kids that these topics are important, even if they are hard to talk about.

BIG STORIES SPARK PARENT ACTION

News about school safety, online predators, or even an upcoming flu epidemic prompts parents to move a topic into the forefront of their efforts. Sometimes we are already prepared, but sometimes the news is shocking, and we are left feeling like we are not prepared if the same problem were to hit our family.

In September 2016, allegations of sexual assault on hundreds of gymnasts, including Olympic gymnasts, came to light. Larry Nassar, a physician, abused them during medical treatment sessions. Many of the athletes were minors at the time of the abuse. Coaches and other staff members were accused as well.

Sadly, there are many other stories about children being sexually abused. As parents, we are left scrambling to add more strategies to try to cover the holes we see in our approach.

At what age do you feel you should discuss sexual assault and safety practices with your children? Our pediatrician told me that I needed to start the conversation before my kids began school, which was preschool age. Yikes was my first thought!

While the information I gave my preschoolers was very basic and based on advice from my pediatrician, it was not an easy conversation.

More details can be added each year as kids get older and more mature.

 At what age will you start talking with kids about sexual safety? How can you keep it age-appropriate? How often will you revisit the topic? Plan this out and know what you want to say because it is hard to talk to kids about this. You don't want to alarm them, but they must be aware and know what they can do if they have a problem. Kids need to be prepared and know what to do if something feels wrong to them.

Your pediatrician can help you with age-appropriate resources to use. Check in with your parenting network to see how they have handled this topic. They may have good resources for you to look into.

Movies always pushed many social topics onto our parenting list of issues to discuss with the kids. The rating system is a good base, but there always seemed to be a few surprises in movies that we were not ready for. Maybe a new curse word, or a sticky situation that we had not touched base on yet.

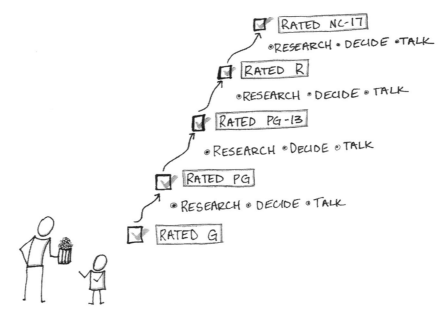

As mentioned in the technology chapter, websites and apps, such as Plugged In and Common Sense Media, provide the details of what is in a movie. This allows parents to decide against seeing a movie or opt to talk with kids about questionable elements in the film.

SHARING HERITAGE, CULTURE, AND RELIGION

Handing down traditions, recipes, crafts, dances, prayers, and rites of passage invites kids to not only bond within the family but within a community.

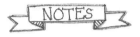 As a parenting team, decide on what cultural or religious traditions and customs you would like to share as a family. If you come from different backgrounds, you may need to determine if you want to share all aspects of both backgrounds or merge some traditions or leave some out. What parts of your family traditions and culture would you like to pass on to your children?

Celebrating subcultures can help your kids share customs as members of a bigger society. Broaden the horizons of your family and learn about other cultures and heritages. Step out and visit festivals, parades, and events that share other people's traditions in your community.

Check out a local Oktoberfest celebration, Cinco de Mayo block party, a Dr. Martin Luther King Jr. march, a parade, or a local church bazaar. Try new foods; learn about other people.

Celebrate the traditions within your family, as well as the diversity in society.

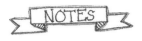 In what ways would you like to learn about other cultures and people in your community?

USE THE IDEAS PROCESS TO MANAGE SOCIAL TOPICS

What are the social issues that you are imagining are on the horizon for your parenting? Start developing your strategies by researching, observing others, and brainstorming. Enlist other parents from your parenting network to divide and conquer these issues. Write down your solutions and strategies in the appropriate age sections of your Parenting Roadmap. Use your solutions and be sure to update, or tweak, as needed.

Like the technology chapter, this section will show different social issues in each step of the IDEAS process.

IMAGINE CONCERNS — SOCIAL

Imagining your concerns ahead of time and planning for them will help you get prepared.

Many parents dread the "Where do babies come from?" conversations with kids, but there is much more to those conversations as kids mature into puberty. Be honest with kids. This means leaving the stork out of the conversation and getting to the facts.

What are your thoughts on teens meeting other teens online, or on dating apps? What are acceptable ways to ask someone on a date, and what are acceptable ways to turn someone down?

Parents are finding themselves defining bullying and sexual harassment to kids as a new norm. Where are the lines drawn between teasing and bullying, or between flirting and harassment? How do these topics look in person versus online?

 In your Parenting Roadmap, make a list of difficult social issues that you want to plan ahead for conversations.

DEVELOP STRATEGIES — SOCIAL

Now that you have a list of social concerns, you can develop strategies by researching, observing, and brainstorming. The good news is that society is easy to observe and research. We see and hear about it every day in the news, or by walking down the street or doing an online search.

You can also look to museums, galleries, and festivals to find strategies for getting along in society or talking about hard topics. Artifacts, murals, dances, and stories all can help teach lessons about society and its norms.

How can you take what you observe and form a plan to educate your kids?

RED RIBBON WEEK

Many parents worry about their kids and substance abuse. Whether it's alcohol, tobacco, vaping, pot, or any number of other drugs, there is a lot for parents to talk about with their kids, and keep track of.

Parents can observe teachers during Red Ribbon Week, which is the "Just Say No to Drugs and Alcohol" campaign that occurs in elementary schools. Typically, during these weeks, schools offer resources and discussions about substance abuse at age-appropriate levels. It is a good time for parents to develop strategies for talking with kids at home as well.

Find out what the kids learned at school and expand on any subject if needed. School counselors and psychologists can recommend good substance abuse resources that are age-appropriate.

As you come across good resources, books, websites, and classes that help parents learn about these topics, keep track of them in your Parenting Roadmap so you can refer to them.

ENLIST OTHERS — SOCIAL

When it comes to changing social norms, enlist others to help you develop parenting strategies. Sometimes, we may need to talk with another adult. We need to vent. We need to share the shock we feel over a new social issue.

Conversations with other parents can help us release the tension from a shocking situation. We can begin to sort out our feelings and develop plans and solutions.

Eighteen-year-olds are considered adults by law. While many eighteen-year-olds can handle the legal responsibilities and decisions at this point, some are not quite mature enough and may still need your advice.

Seventeen-year-olds tend to look toward their eighteenth birthday not as a time when they are taking on more adult responsibility, such as voting and becoming legally responsible for their decisions, but more as a time of fun and the party aspects of adulthood. Things like being able to buy lottery tickets or cigarettes . . . it's more of a *Yay I'm turning eighteen! I can do whatever I want without permission from my parents* attitude. But they need to be prepared for the critical responsibilities that come along with being eighteen.

Prepare your Parenting Roadmap for how you will handle the eighteenth birthday issues. Maybe you are okay with your kids making these choices at eighteen; maybe you are not.

However you feel about these popular issues, plan to talk with your kids ahead of time. Waiting until they turn eighteen may be too late.

TATTOOS, PIERCINGS, AND GAUGES, OH MY!

It's true that many states do not require an eighteen-year-old to get a permission slip signed for tattoos, piercings, and gauges. Many parents are shocked when their son or daughter shows up at home with one or more of these, especially on a return from college.

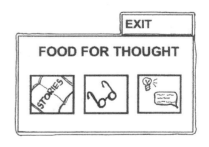

Are you still paying for your child's healthcare? It's a tough one to manage if this is a parenting dilemma for you. You can try to tell them that once they have their own medical coverage, they can choose whatever they want. You can try to show them how much they will pay monthly if they make legal but unhealthy choices, or if their decisions are bothersome to you.

Parents may wish they could turn back the clock to talk about these body-altering decorations. This is a good time to turn to a trusted fellow parent in your parenting network. Maybe you need to vent, or maybe you are looking for advice from a parent who has been in the same position. Either way, enlisting an empathetic parent to talk with can help you work through a surprising situation and maybe help find solutions.

AUTHOR YOUR ROADMAP – SOCIAL

Doctors keep notes between patient visits to help them remember each patient's record of health. It helps them keep track of that patient and their future treatments.

Parents can take notes to keep track of things they learn along the way to use for future siblings. I authored a few notes after my oldest daughter had her thirteen-year-old checkup.

THE THIRTEEN-YEAR-OLD CHECKUP

I remember taking my oldest in for her physical at thirteen, and after talking with her doctor, I went into the waiting room. This is the year the doctor mentioned that unless I have permission from my thirteen-year-old daughter, I would not

have access to her online files anymore after this appointment. What? Thirteen? She's still a kid! I learned the reason this policy is implemented for thirteen-year-olds is in the event of abuse or neglect cases.

All she had to do was sign a release form so that we could continue to have access to her information, which she did.

I talked with her later about this policy. We talked about abuse and how kids may need to ask questions about sex or drugs and do not want their parents or guardians to know. We talked about how we would want her to feel free to ask questions of us, and we would give her honest answers and help her with problems. We discussed that she could also decide to ask her doctor any question, and that would be between her and her doctor.

We wanted to talk with our kids about tough topics and answer any questions they felt comfortable asking us before their doctor checkups. We also wanted to speak with them about how decisions they make could affect the rest of their lives. As parents, we can take the time to help them think about these issues and give them strategies early and before they are put into a situation to need them.

Then when they saw the doctor, we had already talked, and they were prepared to ask the doctor anything else they needed to ask while the topics were fresh in their minds, as well as know that if they wanted to keep the conversation with the doctor private, they could.

These were important points to add to our roadmap.

Solutions for Noteworthy Parenting — Social

Having your solutions ready, even though you know there will be changes to some of these social norms in the future, still puts you ahead in the game of parenting. You will have a good foundation. You may not need to change anything in your plan, or you may need to make updates.

One area that seems like it never changes is teaching kids how to spend and save money, but even the topic of money management evolves.

Helping kids learn to pay bills online and use money-sharing apps are a couple of topics to consider.

The use of credit cards is also a topic you may want to cover. As a society, credit card debt weighs heavy on many people. Some people feel kids should have credit cards in order to build up their credit scores, while others think it is too big of a spending temptation.

CREDIT CARDS AND THE EIGHTEEN-YEAR-OLD

Companies put a huge marketing effort into enticing college kids to sign up for credit cards. They send emails, junk mail, and set up tables of cool giveaways on campus. They are tempting and convincing.

Are your kids ready to handle the temptation of spending with credit cards?

I managed a little watch store when I was first married. Many of the employees in my store were high school and college kids. I was always sad when they graduated from high school and they would go off to college. I missed them, and it was harder to fill in the schedule.

One year, one of my new freshman employees called me on Halloween in tears, begging for as many hours as I could give her over Thanksgiving and winter break. She had signed up for a few credit cards the first week of school and had gone on quite a spending spree over the following few weeks. She shopped for clothes, dorm items, and ate out at restaurants, even though she had free access to the school cafeteria. She built up close to one thousand dollars in debt. Her parents found out, and she was in deep trouble.

While I was delighted to give her the hours, my heart broke for her. That was a hard lesson to learn. I did not have kids at the time, but it left such a huge impression on me that we made sure to talk about this with our kids.

 How can you mentor the use of credit cards before the credit card companies entice your kid?

Teaching your child adult responsibilities over time will prepare them for the young adult stage. You will feel confident letting them go, rather than fretting that they do not know how to handle things. They will still need coaching from you, and they will make mistakes (as will you), but it's better than holding their hands because they are completely inexperienced. Spread out your plan in your roadmap so that piece by piece, age by age, bit by bit, you can prepare them.

There are no fixed points in which each stage of childhood moves to the next. Society may try to impose guidelines, but only you and your kids know what feels right as you raise your family.

SUMMARY

- CHAPTER 5 -
- SOCIAL CLIMATE

PARTYING · CULTURE · RELIGIONS · BIRTH CONTROL · ABSTINENCE · MARIJUANA · DRUGS · VOTE · TATTOO · PIERCING · BULLIES · RATED R · MOVIES · LANGUAGE · VIOLENCE

· TOUGH TALKS · PARENTING SOCIAL CHANGES · BIG NEWS · PARENT ACTION ·

IDEAS

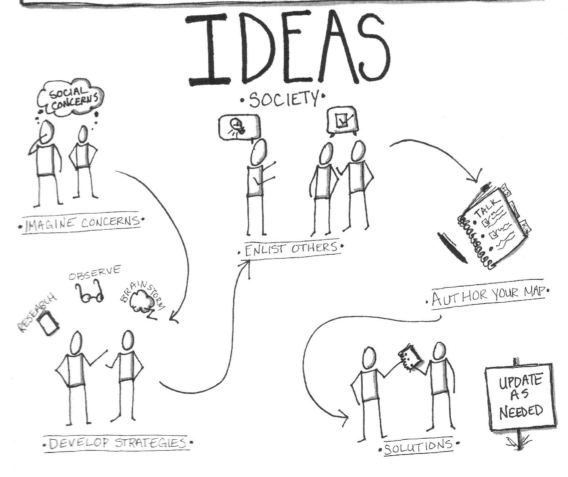

· SOCIETY ·

· IMAGINE CONCERNS ·

· ENLIST OTHERS ·

· AUTHOR YOUR MAP ·

OBSERVE · RESEARCH · BRAINSTORM

· DEVELOP STRATEGIES ·

· SOLUTIONS ·

UPDATE AS NEEDED

CHAPTER 6

Parents—A Look at ourselves

"Done properly, parenting is a heroic act . . . done properly."
—Edna Mode, Incredibles 2

Being responsible for the physical, emotional, cultural, and intellectual development of little human beings is a heavy burden to carry. All parents feel pressure to be perfect. The margin for error between doing it right and messing it up seems small.

People never really understand what it takes to be a parent until they become one—until we are in the chaos, losing sleep, and dealing with the shock of it all.

So as parents, we walk around carrying this burden of responsibility along with the instinctual, deep love for our kids. When things go right, we feel like superheroes, but when things go wrong, we feel defeated.

So, how do we manage the heroic task of parenting properly?

PARENTING STAMINA

Stamina is typically a word we hear when talking about physical exercise, but parenting stamina is the grit required to manage the chaos. It is enduring moment after moment in tough times.

It is enduring a lack of sleep.

It is enduring the auto-repeat for giving instructions.

It is enduring mistakes, bad choices, and the messy learning process of little human beings.

It is enduring the stomach flu as it passes from one family member to the next.

It is enduring the eye-rolling of teenagers.

It is the physical and emotional dedication to loving and mentoring your kids.

The parental muscles are pumping, and like a heartbeat, parents fall into the rhythm of their system, day after day, year after year, until one day they realize their kids are adults.

But what is your system? It's your trusty roadmap. It is there to keep you strong on the journey.

Parenting stamina is needed to mentor your kids into adulthood. It's in the rhythm of providing for, teaching, and eventually letting go of tasks

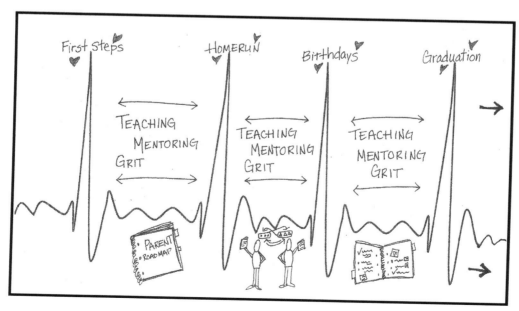

step by step so that over time, your parenting work pays off. Your kids become independent one task at a time.

It is in the endurance and dedication to the daily grit that parenting happens. It's in the work, the teaching, the mentoring to give your child a full, well-rounded life.

Those moments of parenting problem-solving are the basis for creating your Noteworthy Parenting Roadmap. Being prepared will enhance your stamina and enable you to look back as your kids become adults and know that you did the very best parenting you could.

You created a parenting plan, implemented it, and that stamina minimized regret and allowed you to focus on the joyful times of parenting.

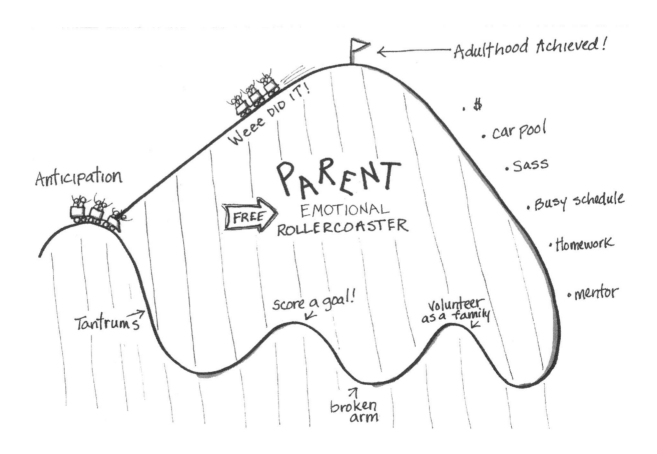

PARENTING: AN EMOTIONAL ENDEAVOR

Buckle your seatbelt: parents embark on a rollercoaster of emotions. What are some of those emotions? What will you feel over the years?

Love, stress, pride, joy, worry, frustration, embarrassment, anticipation, exhaustion, fear, anger, shock, surprise, annoyance, and many others!

Emotions can be anticipated or unforeseen.

What sparks all these emotions?

Spilled milk, first steps, birthdays, bullies, kindergarten, team sports, vacations, a trip to the principal's office, prom, graduations, and weddings, to name a few.

You never know when those emotions are going to hit you.

Some people tear up as they leave their child for their first day of school; others do not. Some people get emotional as they watch their kids play soccer or the piano. Some people get mama bear angry when someone has wronged their child, while others can keep a level head during such moments.

When your teenager misses a curfew, what will your emotional state be? Worry? Frustration? Anger? Maybe they had a good reason, and you're just happy they are okay. However, when it happens for the fifth time in a month, what will your emotions be?

It's hard to take the time and energy to sort through your emotions, which string together, task after task until you hit your pillow at night completely exhausted.

Be prepared and have tissues handy; it's okay to cry.

Be prepared to lose your temper; that's okay too. Cool off, revisit the topic with the kids, apologize as needed, and move on.

Be prepared to be authentic, honest, and open, because your kids will learn how to deal with their emotions by watching you.

Create family goals, plan for them, and achieve them so they have no regrets. Prepare early for kids' weddings, college, or moving out, so you are prepared not only financially but emotionally.

Make sure you are taking care of your physical health too! Get exercise. Eat healthy. Meet up with friends.

If you are struggling with emotions that you may need help with, seek out counseling or a therapist to help you.

Nobody's perfect; you will make mistakes. All you can do is learn from them and move forward.

"Do the best you can until you learn better, then do better!" —Maya Angelou

Sometimes we have superhero moments, and sometimes we don't. We are parents, doing the best we can.

Here are a few Food for Thought Exits for dealing with parenting emotions such as stress, anger, worry, and anxiety.

MONEY, MONEY, MONEY

Money can be the source of a lot of stress for parents. In the beginning, parents plan for the added diaper cost on the grocery bill or the savings accounts for college, but there are growing costs  on parent budgets these days, which can add stress to the family.

When I was growing up, the only cost to my parents for public education was school supplies.

As my kids moved through the school years, school funding got tighter and tighter with the passing of each year. One high school year, my son's course fees and extracurricular fees were over $1,000.

Parents are responsible for more and more of the school supply costs, like printing and computer paper fees, book purchases, testing fees, calculators, technology fees, bus service, parking permits, and art class supplies.

The cost of participating in extracurricular activities is adding up for parents as well: tournament entrance fees, transportation fees, team dinners, equipment rentals, uniforms, and camps. These fees are not usually too bad in elementary school, but as kids hit middle and high school, they add up.

A budget line item for school fees is a smart move.

What are other hidden costs parents may encounter?

Fundraising events and items. Often, parents are asked to make donations for bake sales, silent auctions, or to support activities with decorations, supplies, or food. Parents are asked to fundraise by selling predetermined products like wrapping paper or candy bars. How much will you end up purchasing to meet a targeted goal or to help support the cause?

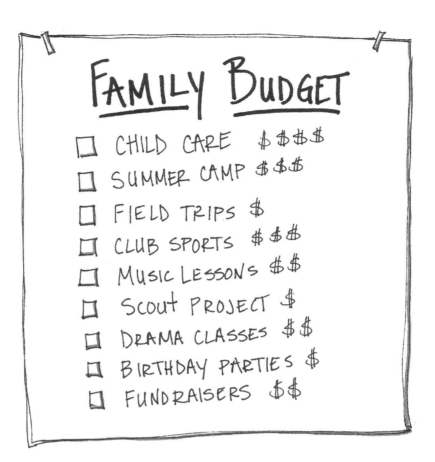

FAMILY BUDGET

- ☐ CHILD CARE $$$$
- ☐ SUMMER CAMP $$$
- ☐ FIELD TRIPS $
- ☐ CLUB SPORTS $$$
- ☐ MUSIC LESSONS $$
- ☐ SCOUT PROJECT $
- ☐ DRAMA CLASSES $$
- ☐ BIRTHDAY PARTIES $
- ☐ FUNDRAISERS $$

NOTES Start a list of budget items you will need to prepare for.

BORROWING OR STEALING?

As kids get older and become more like adults in physical size as well as capabilities, parents' items become useful and appealing to kids.

FOOD FOR THOUGHT

My daughters were able to wear some of my clothes as they became middle schoolers. Once in a while, they would wear my scarves, shoes, and jewelry.

The boys may need to borrow an occasional tie from Dad or borrow his favorite NHL hockey sweater for jersey day at school.

Maybe they need to borrow your laptop?

Then there is the infamous longing to borrow the car.

It can be fun and budget-friendly to share clothes and accessories with your kids. Sharing laptops and cars also saves the family a lot of money.

It's all peachy until it becomes less of a "polite borrowing process" and more of the "stealing and never returning process" or the "assuming I could use it process."

This happened with one of my daughters. She would take things from my closet, wear them, and forget to clean and return them. I kindly reminded her to ask first. Annoyed, I then reminded her again to ask first. Finally, I angrily told her she was not allowed to borrow my clothes anymore, and then repeated this step a few more times.

Each time she would chuckle and say she would stop. She did not, and my annoyance and frustration levels were bubbling up.

At a family dinner, I was mentioning this aggravating dilemma to my siblings. I explained that I would like to pack up a bunch of her clothes and give them away to teach her a lesson. I was at the end of my rope. They all agreed and were on board sharing their ideas.

As we continued to talk, my husband suggested that we should pack up her clothes and take them down to the base-ment instead of giving them away. All of us were on board with this. Even my mild-tempered brother-in-law was part of the movement to teach this lesson!

It felt like we were wrapped up in a bit of a mob mentality. They all wanted me to text pictures of the trash bags and wanted updates, but it was good to have the parental support needed to take on this melodramatic "grab your torch and pitchfork, let's kill the Beast" Beauty and the Beast-type of teaching lesson.

We got home from dinner that night, and while my daughter was still at work, I grabbed a few trash bags and filled them with her clothes — from her bedroom floor, drawers, and closet.

I took the bags to the basement and waited for her to come home. When she entered her room and saw her clothes missing (probably shocked that she could see the carpet on her bedroom floor), she knew something was up and came right away to see me. I asked her how it felt to have missing clothes. I told her that's how I felt when getting ready for work in the morning and I couldn't find the clothes that I wanted to wear.

I told her where her clothes were, and she quietly headed to the basement to retrieve them. I suggested that she think about how she would change as she was putting each item away. I wanted her to think about how I felt searching for my clothes only to find them wadded up in the corner of her room, dirty and wrinkled.

All of a sudden, the situation wasn't so funny to her anymore. The plan worked, and I should've done something more concrete like this sooner. It is a great example of enlisting others (from the IDEAS section) for ideas and teaching a lesson rather than continuing to repeat the same nagging, unsuccessful threats over and over again. She was not allowed to borrow my things again, and she respected that.

I was relieved of the frustration that was looming over the relationship between my daughter and me.

Borrowing or stealing causes frustration for parents. Typically, this happens with teenagers who want to borrow the car, clothes, makeup, or anything their hearts desire.

Sharing clothes, cars, and items works well when the borrower respects the owner and asks.

PARENTING PEER PRESSURE

Parenting peer pressure is when parents allow themselves to be affected by social pressure to take a certain action, adopt certain values, make decisions, or otherwise conform to be accepted. Where does this social pressure come from? It comes from other parents, family members, and the media.

We experienced parenting peer pressure as we were raising our kids. But what helped us is that we had our Parenting Roadmap in place. We had thought through our parenting decisions and were confident in our plan.

We knew how much money we could afford for holidays, birthdays, and college per kid. We researched the content of PG-13 movies before kids were allowed to watch them, even at thirteen, fourteen, and fifteen. Each kid could pick two extracurricular activities for the year. All electronic devices had to be turned in and recharged in our room overnight, including cell phones, until the kids graduated from high school.

One of the rules in our plan that my husband and I had to explain the most was our policy on no slumber parties. We were happy to come and pick our kids up as the party was winding down for the night, but they weren't allowed to stay the night. As these invites would come along, my husband or I would try to touch base with the parents ahead of time to thank them for the invite let them know our system.

Most parents had no problem with this, but some thought we were crazy. We had several reasons for our no-slumber-party system, we stuck to it, and even had a few other parents adopt the system for their families.

No two families are exactly the same. You don't have to do things the same as other parents. We are all trying to do the best we can to raise our kids and keep them safe.

Respecting another family's rules even though they are different from yours shows your kids that you respect the diversity of other families.

It will be good for kids to see you set the example, as they enter into peer pressure situations. They can see how it works and have the confidence to follow the rules or stand up for what works for them.

JUST SAY NO TO PARENTING PRESSURE

So, if you're feeling overwhelmed as a parent because you've been trying to keep up with other families, start setting your own rules and lighten your load.

If your calendar is overbooked, fix that! What activities can you eliminate?

Decide ahead of time how much you will spend on gifts, activities, and fundraising.

If you can't afford an expensive activity, have your child help earn the money, or request money instead of gifts, if they want it badly enough.

If the content in movies or video games concerns you, set up rules and parameters that make you feel in charge of your parenting.

Attentive, engaged, and loving parents are what kids need.

So, don't worry if you are doing it the same as what other parents are doing—follow your gut instinct and your good judgment. Write down your systems and rules; get on the same page. Have confidence in your decisions.

Who knows? Your confidence may help other parents you know to start thinking about their parenting and create their own roadmap.

Parenting shouldn't be a competition of who is doing it the best, who can spend the most money, or have the busiest calendar. As I like to say, it's not about keeping up with the Joneses but about teaming up with the Joneses.

VOLUNTEERING

With so many funding cuts over the years, many schools and organizations rely on volunteers to succeed. This has become a valuable dimension for parents to consider.

Volunteering benefits you as a parent by setting an example of community service for your kids. It also allows you to meet the kids, teachers, coaches, and other parents that your kids interact with. You can share your expertise about activities or do it to have fun and enjoy your community.

Thinking ahead can help you ensure you are selecting a volunteer opportunity that is right for you and your family. When choosing volunteer jobs, consider how much time you would like to commit and what type of help you would enjoy offering. This consideration will help you say yes to the activities you enjoy and avoid overcommitting yourself.

Would you like to coach a soccer team that practices twice a week and has games on Saturdays for six weeks? Do you prefer to practice reading with first-graders for two hours every Tuesday morning? Maybe grading student work at home is more your cup of tea? Some parents enjoy being scout leaders, while others prefer to work the concessions at the high school football games.

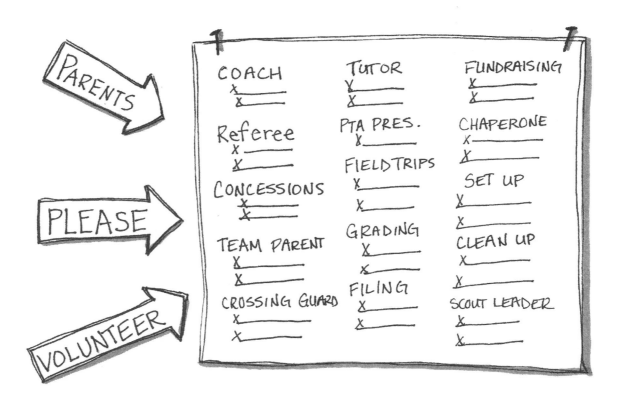

There is a huge need for good, reliable help in the community, and often not enough people volunteer. Commit to what you enjoy and the amount of time you can offer. Do not feel guilty and overcommit yourself. You will have years to volunteer as your kids grow. Don't burn yourself out too soon.

If a program has to be canceled due to lack of help, then maybe next time more people will come forward to help. Do not feel obligated to fill all the gaps yourself.

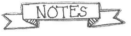 What type of volunteering would you like to do? What volunteering activities do you not want to do? How much time and when can you volunteer?

TAKE A BREAK!

Yep! Parents need a break.

Why? Parents need time to recharge, think, laugh, and talk with other adults. Who are we kidding? Parents need a little fun without worrying about chasing or entertaining their kids once in a while. It's good for the parent's mind, body, and soul.

When parents take a break, the kids have fun too! They get to have a babysitter who will play with them and maybe even give them parent-approved (or unapproved) treats.

Whether you leave the kids for a few hours or take a little getaway, you will come back refreshed, and your kids will be refreshed too. You may even find that you miss each other.

Arranging for babysitters is not always easy, but well worth the effort. Make this task easier as a parenting team by creating a list of your babysitters.

Who can you put on your babysitter list? Family, friends, neighbors, and teenagers all make good babysitters.

Do you need to find babysitters? Check with your parenting network of friends for recommendations. Neighborhood newsletters and child-care apps may have lists of sitters and their qualifications. Your local American Red Cross may have a list of graduates from their Certified Teen Babysitter class.

Be sure to meet and interview babysitters that are new to your family. Have the kids around to meet new babysitters and help pick the ones they like.

 Create a list of babysitters you feel comfortable with along with their contact information and their rate of pay in your Parenting Roadmap.

Talk with your parenting team about what each parent would like to have time to do. Maybe one parent would like to work out an hour each day, or go back to school to earn a degree, take a painting class, or go to yoga. The other parent may like time to occasionally meet up with friends or start a new hobby.

Maybe you both want to go out to see a movie, travel, or take time to sit

and discuss your Parenting Roadmap or other family needs.

Set goals and schedules so that your break time does not fall through the cracks, and you find yourself burning out.

PRESENCE INSTEAD OF PRESENTS

My husband and I decided after a few years of parenting that we would prefer date nights, or a yearly long weekend, over getting each other gifts. We did not need to accumulate more items. He started traveling more for his job, and we felt like we needed to find a way to take a break that helped us stay connected.

Thankfully, my younger siblings, as well as grandparents on both sides, were helpful babysitters. This allowed us to catch up, rejuvenate, and have fun at the same time. When the kids were younger, we went once a year; as they got older, we would go once around my March birthday and once around his October birthday.

I have known friends who take a day off of work to spend time together while their kids are at school or in day care.

Thinking creatively, you can come up with solutions to afford the money and time to catch a break!

Make sure to take the time to think about yourself as a parent. How can you plan to be the best you can be as a parent? Notice that I did not say perfect. By taking a look at yourself and taking care of yourself, you can make plans to be an amazing parent. You will be able to look back when your kids are grown and say, I may not have been perfect, but I did the best I could, and I was a superhero parent!

CHAPTER 7

YDY—Your Unique Parenting Roadmap

"The delicate balance of mentoring someone is not creating them in your own image but giving them the opportunity to create themselves."
—Steven Spielberg

YDY (YOU DO YOU) NOTETAKING

While writing this book and sharing the ideas for creating a Parenting Roadmap, people kept asking me what the system is. Over my years of parenting and teaching, I have learned that each person has a method and system that works well for them.

Humans are unique! We create differently, think differently, and, well, we use information differently.

I have seen kids and adults struggle to learn and use good information because the notetaking method or the system wasn't user-friendly, or they were so focused on getting the process perfected that they could not remember the "meat" of the information.

We get caught up in copying the exact process, thinking that is where the secret to success lies, when in reality, the success lies in the content and how it can work for you. The keys are your ideas, plans, goals, routines,

and the notes you create; it's not in the method you choose.

The companion Noteworthy Parenting Roadmap is set up for you to get started right away on these topics:

- Infant
- Toddler
- Preschool
- Primary Grades (K–2)
- Secondary Grades (3–5)
- Middle School (6–8)
- High School (9–12)
- Young Adult

These are added pages to keep you on top of your extra parenting duties:

FAMILY GOALS: Write down the goals you have as a family and break them down into smaller pieces, or keep a schedule so you stay on track toward achieving your goals!

TRADITIONS, CUSTOMS, AND HOLIDAYS: To keep notes of who is hosting Thanksgiving dinner this year, or a list of Santa's gift-giving parameters, and maybe a note about how much the Tooth Fairy leaves for a tooth.

SPECIAL EVENTS: Details for birthdays, graduations, and weddings. This helps when younger siblings come along so you can remember how much you spent and the general details of events.

GIFTS GIVEN: A great sheet to keep track of how much you spent on holidays, birthdays, graduations, and weddings, not only for your kids, but for nieces, nephews, and friends.

CONTRACTS: Keep track of loans you give your kids for extras, or for checking college grades, or if kids move back in. You add the stipulations and details, and both parties sign and date it.

PARENT PAGES: Keep track of babysitters, your adult goals, and lists of how you would like to spend your "kid-free" time.

You can also use these pages to create a notebook for your roadmap, or you can use the categories to label pages in a spiral notebook if that works better for you.

Maybe you prefer a notes app or a Word file for your notes. Use whatever system works best for you.

YDY (YOU DO YOU) CONTENT

In this book and online, I share ideas, thoughts, and topics to inspire you to think ahead about parenting topics, issues, and stages.

Reflect on the most important and useful aspects of the Parenting Roadmap for you and your parenting team. It is then that the content becomes an empowering tool for your parenting and family life.

In the beginning of this book, I mentioned that there are almost 80,000 books listed on Amazon about parenting. There are countless classes and seminars, and you can access advice from elders, family, and friends. Your resources are endless.

Through my parenting career as well as my teaching career, I found that most resources had good advice to take away, as well as advice and ideas that didn't work well for me.

As you come across various resources, these are likely to have good tips for you to use, as well as some you won't utilize at all. You choose.

YDY (YOU DO YOU) PARENTING ROADMAP MAINTENANCE

Prioritize creating your roadmap because it will empower you, reduce regrets, enhance confidence, and encourage consistency and focus in your parenting.

Set aside time to monitor your plan's effectiveness. Do you need to update or tweak a part of the plan? Are you ready to plan for the upcoming stages?

Keep your Parenting Roadmap well-maintained and current!

Remember, you are the parent; you get to choose what goes in your Parenting Roadmap.

Here is the point where I let go, and you take over.

Think of the great Nike motto, "Just do it." It's not about being pretty and it's not about being perfect.

It's about the power in your parenting plan . . . Think it . . . Note it . . . Parent it.

SUMMARY

• CHAPTER 7 •

YDY

• YOUR UNIQUE PARENTING ROADMAP •

BEGIN!!

Index: Food for Thought Exits

To make creating your parenting roadmap easier, check out the Noteworthy Parenting Roadmap: A Companion Journal to Note Your Best Parenting IDEAS.

It's set up with all of the categories you need to get started on your journey!

Available on Amazon or at NoteworthyParenting.com

Acknowledgments

A great big thank you to Tim and Jean LeDuc, my parents, and Bill and Jeanie Buchtel, my in-laws, who set the parenting standard but allowed us to find our unique parenting path. To my husband, Darin, and my kids, Abbey (Ryan), Jake, Emily, and Jason for all of the cheerleading they gave me to complete this book.

Thank you to all of our friends and family who have been with us as a part of our parenting network, with a special thanks to our small church community: Mike, Leslie, Kurt, Denine, Jeff, Anita, Rich, and Madeline. To Jayne Basford who critiqued several drafts and discussed them with me over countless cups of chai tea.

To my beta readers who gave me insightful and humorous feedback, Annie Foppe, Abbey Giedraitis, Ryan Giedraitis, Malia Golden, Katie Kassowitz, Ron Konrath, Trina Konrath, Jon LeDuc, Katie LeDuc, Lindsey LeDuc, and Greg Smoczyk.

To Chris Chopyak for the inspiration to tackle the illustrations. To Alexandra O'Connell, my wise and gentle editor, who bulletproofed my work with precision. To Polly Letofsky, who mentored me to publication with her groovy style. Lastly, a special thanks to Victoria Wolf, who magically turned my writing and illustrations into this nifty little book.

About the Author

Kristin Buchtel and her husband live in Westminster, Colorado, close to their four adult children. After receiving her master's degree in elementary education, Kristin taught in K–3 classrooms for over ten years and was the recipient of two District Values Awards.

Throughout her parenting career of staying home with her kids, years of volunteering, classroom teaching, and doing home day care, she experienced and observed a lot of parental angst over parenting perfection. This led Kristin and her husband to create their own plan as they were approaching their kids' teen years. Their plan wasn't pretty, but it was the beginning of their most powerful parenting tool, their Parenting Roadmap. Kristin's passion is to inspire parents to find their own unique ways of parenting by taking advice and tips that resonate with their style, noting them, and parenting by them.

You can find more information and food for thought at
www.noteworthyparenting.com

Made in the USA
San Bernardino, CA
31 January 2020